HOW TO
COACH YOUTH
BASEBALL
SO EVERY KID WINS

HOW TO COACH YOUTH BASEBALL
SO EVERY KID WINS

JEFF OURVAN

Foreword by Orlando Cepeda

Skyhorse Publishing

Skyhorse Publishing books may be purchased in bulk at special discounts for sales promotion, corporate gifts, fund-raising, or educational purposes. Special editions can also be created to specifications. For details, contact the Special Sales Department, Skyhorse Publishing, 307 West 36th Street, 11th Floor, New York, NY 10018 or info@skyhorsepublishing.com.

Skyhorse® and Skyhorse Publishing® are registered trademarks of Skyhorse Publishing, Inc.®, a Delaware corporation.

Visit our website at www.skyhorsepublishing.com.

10 9 8 7 6 5 4 3 2 1

Library of Congress Cataloging-in-Publication Data is available on file.
ISBN: 978-1-61608-357-1

Printed in China

For Jake, Kevin, and Vince

CONTENTS »

"It's what you learn after you know it all that counts."

—Earl Weaver

FOREWORD »

There have been two very large influences in my life. The first, of course, is baseball.

My father, Pedro, was the greatest Puerto Rican baseball player of his day, and he played alongside legends such as Satchel Paige, Josh Gibson, and Roy Campanella. But those were the days before Jackie Robinson, and my father had no hope of ever making it to the big leagues or of earning a real living through the game. In fact, throughout his entire baseball career, and my youth, my family was extremely poor.

My father played baseball for one reason: He loved the game. As kids, my brothers and I also played for the same reason. Starting at around age nine, it was all I ever wanted to do, morning till night, seven days a week, all year round. But when I was thirteen I almost walked away from the game forever. There was a team then that I very much wanted to play for, but I had to come up with a registration fee and my family didn't have the money. It was all of fifty cents. So my mother, seeing me in tears, had to work extra to scrape it together, and finally I registered for the team. I showed up at our first practice. There was a uniform there for everyone except me. It turned out that I wasn't good enough to have been chosen. I was devastated. There were no words of encouragement to me from the coach. Instead, I was ignored and left to drag my poor self home.

I decided right there that I would never play baseball again. For two years I didn't even touch a bat and ball. If it wasn't for my brother's encouragement, and also my father's wise patience, I may never have come back. In my case, of course, that would have meant no World Series championship, no MVP, no All-Star Game appearances and no Baseball Hall of Fame. I sometimes wonder whether that coach, back then, might have handled that situation with me in a more thoughtful way.

The second large influence in my life has been my faith in Buddhism. Among the many things Buddhism has taught me is that everyone is inherently equal, and everyone is worthy of respect. In other words, each person has something valuable to contribute if given the chance.

This very fine and necessary book couples the beauty of baseball together with an emphasis on consideration toward each child who plays the game. It values the importance of winning. And it offers all the tools and basic baseball coaching skills to lead your team toward that goal. At the same time, it teaches how to cherish every member of your team so that you not only win as a team but enable each child to create a winning experience in life through the game.

Who knows? With some encouragement, that kid batting at the bottom of your lineup, like me, may someday be a World Champion, too.

Orlando Cepeda
Member, National Baseball Hall of Fame
Author, *Baby Bull: From Hardball to Hard Time and Back*

THE MEANING OF WINNING

This is an instructional guide for youth baseball managers and coaches who unashamedly want their teams to win. It's also a book for those who accept the notion that they can't do this unless their least able players become a crucial part of that winning team.

There are hundreds of thousands of volunteer youth baseball coaches throughout the United States, and most, understandably, are in it because they want to spend time playing baseball with their own kids. But the position of manager or coach—from the perspective of any child between the ages of seven and twelve who, more often than not, lives and dies for baseball—is also one of significant responsibility to all the players on the team. A good or bad coach will make or break the untested baseball player's experience. It's as inspiring to witness a new player improve his or her game and feel victorious as a result of the patience and respect shown by a good coach as it is heartbreaking to see a once-enthusiastic child who sours on the sport because his or her coach was a jerk.

Most volunteer coaches, of course, are good, well-meaning people and they're almost always baseball fans too. The vast majority have children of their own on their teams. Some may have even planned to have kids just for the opportunity to someday coach youth baseball! Many coaches struggle mightily to balance yet another time-consuming activity in the midst of a heavy work schedule and other family, religious, and community obligations. It's not easy to get away with leaving work at 4 PM two to four times a week, over a three to four month period, to hit fungoes to a bunch of ten-year-olds, let alone sacrificing one's Saturday and Sunday mornings in the spring. No one who does this need be criticized or disparaged for their baseball know-how, or lack thereof, when he or she honestly cares about the children on his or her team. But the fact remains that youth baseball coaching, for many, is a first-time experience. While many coaches understand how baseball is played, fewer perceive the proper approaches to youth baseball in particular, and still fewer understand how to create an environment in which all the players are certain that they've won.

Anyone who regularly watches or participates in the thousands upon thousands of organized baseball programs nationwide has observed two coaching archetypes: the win-at-all-costs manager, and the winning-is-not-the-point manager.

The win-at-all-costs manager is typically out for his or her own glory. This coach often shouts at umpires, opposing managers, his own players, and sometimes even the players on the other team. His relatively talented son or daughter is featured at the expense of the lesser players. His most inexperienced players are exiled to the bench or, if they're lucky, the outfield corners, and he considers the bottom of his lineup as something that he just has to get through. He regularly criticizes his players after a loss—a time when children hear nothing but blame. He is invariably the one coach most knowledgeable about the rules and regulations of his respective league, and he doesn't hesitate to agitate for enforcement of even the most obscure rule in order to secure a forfeit against a team that just beat his pants off on the field. The best interests of the children in the league are subsumed by his imperious drive to win. His players sometimes win trophies but are not especially happy. Many parents disparage him behind his back.

In contrast, the winning-is-not-the-point manager is a heck of a nice guy. For him or her, every player is outstanding, and everyone gets the privilege of playing each position—sometimes even in the same game. This manager praises every strikeout as much as every hit, even where the kid has done nothing but strike out throughout the entire season. Practices are squeezed into a half hour before the regularly scheduled game. The score and the standings never matter. What's more important is his positional rotation, even if it's time for a player who can't catch a baseball to play first base and potentially injure him or herself. Sometimes the winning-is-not-the-point manager changes his team's field positions after every out (e.g., everyone shifts one position to the right). There's no pressure in any of his matches, his best pitcher pitches one inning every three games, his best hitter sometimes bats last in the lineup, his worst hitter first, the umpire's never wrong, and it's always a beautiful day for base-ball. Parents enjoy the babysitting privileges of having this sort of manager take their sons or daughters off their hands for two hours at a time. Many of his players disparage him behind his back.

Neither of these approaches is effective. What you need, and the reason you're reading this book in the first place, is a fun method for coaching youth baseball by which you're happy and winning; each of your players, without exception—from the talented to the inex-perienced ones, are challenged but also have a great time; and their parents not only largely stay out of your hair but end up sharing with you sincere words of praise and cool gift certificates as end-of-the-season tokens of appreciation.

The bottom line—whether or not it's politically correct—is that kids want to win. But even more fundamentally, they want to be treated with respect. Ten-year-olds know when a win is hollow, when it's achieved by a technicality as opposed to having prevailed on the field. They don't want to hear how great their swing was when they strikeout for the third straight time. Ten-year-olds also know pretty quickly when they're being disproportionately benched, disregarded at practices, disfavored to the advantage of the coaches' children and made to feel less than an equal part of the team—whether or not they or their parents ever express it. Just as keenly, a ten-year-old who has struggled to play well all season knows when he or she has been unfailingly encouraged, patiently instructed, and considered to be an equal and vital member of the team. And the thrill that that player feels when he or she finally gets a hit, or knocks in an important run later in the season, might even surpass that of the best player when the team wins a championship game. In fact, the joy that radiates from the successes achieved by the most inexperienced players lifts the entire team and, as will be demonstrated throughout this book, is perhaps the key ingredient to victory and certainly the measure of a coach's and a team's success.

A good youth baseball coach handling children between the ages of seven and twelve must realize that he or she isn't coaching baseball—he's coaching *youth baseball*. Youth baseball might resemble baseball, but it's an entirely different game in many ways. Sophisticated baseball drill books written by college or major-league coaches might be useful for youth all-star teams, or for coaches with seasoned fifteen- or sixteen-year-old players, but they're largely useless for brand-new recreational league coaches with younger players who may not even know yet how to catch or throw a ball. Additionally, youth baseball pitchers have detailed pitch counts and walk limits, catchers may or may not have innings limits, all players in uniform are required to be played at least a couple of innings, the ability to take leads and steal bases differs between ages and from league to league, games may be called well before six innings are completed, "mercy rules" often apply and the conditions of the "ball-parks" vary from impeccably groomed grass fields with locker rooms and grandstands to no more than rock- or even glass-strewn urban lots in the shadow of power plants and collapsing steel fences. Most importantly, youth baseball—despite appearances—decidedly is not for the coaches and parents: it's for young people who are either children or on the cusp of adolescence. This reality ought to always be front and center for every youth baseball coach.

Many veteran coaches have various rules that they set forth for their players at the beginning of each season: everyone runs to first base, even on a walk; no one stands in the outfield biting their nails; all infielders must be at ready position before every pitch; players run laps or do extra push-ups if they're late for practices, etc. All of these rules, of course, are fine, especially when tailored to the particular personality of each respective team. However, you really only need the one rule that never fails to nurture respect between the players and among the coaches and players: No player—ever—complains about any other player on the team. Whether it's true or not, and it always depends on the individual child, you should inform your players that you intend to treat them as young men and women (or, for the seven-year-olds, not to treat them like T-ball players). A team is like a body, where each player has a role to play—one is the heart, one the legs, one the arms, etc.—and you never hear your elbow complain about your nose. The privilege of the brain is reserved for the coach. Therefore, any great play made on the field is for the glory of the players involved, but every poor play is the coach's fault, because the coach—or the alleged brain—is the one who put the player in that position, and thus any mistake is the coach's responsibility. Remarkably, each player appreciates and generally observes this rule, from the best player to the least capable. And in the rare cases when they don't, then—and only then—are they benched.

This little speech, at the very first practice, is the opening indication to the relatively more inexperienced players that they're going to have a good time this season. It sparks the flame of self-respect, no matter how small, inherently present in most children who had the guts to try playing organized baseball in the first place, which the attentive coach will continue to fan and build throughout a winning season.

But baseball is a game of failure. The very best hitters reach base less than half the time, and in a ten-team league only one team will come out on top. So what does it mean to win? Finishing in first place, and winning the championship round of playoffs, if there is one in your league, is a fairly good indication of success. But winning is more than that. Winning is courage. It's exhibited by the nine-year-old who you've left on the mound with a tie score and the bases loaded, and who you know—more than he does—can pitch. It's revealed by the last batter in your order who hasn't had a hit all year but manages to get on base to keep a two-out rally going. It's discovered by your regular right fielder, who's been afraid of fly balls all year, but who, with the game on the line, gets under the ball, sticks out his glove and—perhaps with eyes closed—finally makes the catch. And, most importantly, it's within the coach who has the guts and foresight to place his young players in these crucial situations, where they might fail, with the confidence that more times than not they won't.

Particularly for players between the ages of eight and twelve, these are extremely crucial and stressful situations. In many ways, and for many players, this is the most important thing in their world. As much as they may feel horrified and humiliated after blowing a play in front of their peers, they can't even fit their heads in through their front doors after making a play they never really believed they could accomplish. Not only do they feel like winners, but they carry such experiences with them into adolescence and adult life. These are the situations that not only foster winning teams but, more importantly, strong young men and women.

You'll be amazed how hard boys and girls will play for you at the end of the season, in the playoffs, when you've treated them with this level of respect and genuine care throughout the year. It's still a winning coach who's had the irreplaceable pride of being too choked up to even address his or her tearful players after their last playoff game, which was lost by one run, in extra innings, because each of them fought so hard that they weren't even close to resembling the same boys and girls at the start of the season.

Succeeding in the game of baseball takes both tangible and intangible skills. Although understanding young hearts and minds is crucial, these kids still have to learn how to catch and throw the ball to the right base. The ensuing chapters offer detailed skills drills and strategic approaches to base running, batting, throwing and pitching, and fielding, with the general observation that alertness in the field always leads to good at-bats and heads-up play. The skills and recommended approaches included here are time-tested and, moreover, fun. They're designed to teach baseball while keeping young people engaged and excited to participate in practices.

More than even natural skills, though, children need confidence to excel in baseball. Confidence comes, of course, as a result of diligent practice, but the coach, to a considerable extent, also plays a large role in helping his or her players to feel comfortable on the field. The approach to good coaching in some respects isn't a whole lot different from good parenting—if a player is ignored he or she won't thrive; if the player is given attention and feels like an essential part of the team he or she will rise to the challenges on the baseball diamond.

As important as it is to correctly teach fundamental baseball skills, a coach of young children, especially, also has to come to understand what it takes to motivate his or her players to run the bases well, to catch, field and throw, and to hit the ball successfully. Although baseball, on the surface, is a relatively simple game, the proper execution of these fundamentals isn't so straightforward. When it comes to base running, for example, a seemingly easy part of the game, players have to learn how to run through first base on a grounder or pop-up; how to run outside of the base path in preparation for advancing to second base; how and when to take leads; how and when to steal; how to slide; how to break up a double-play; how and when to tag up; and how to read coaching signs, among other skills. And as with other baseball fundamentals, not to mention just about everything else in life, it takes practice to prosper. But what are the keys to a child's mind and heart in helping him or her to run the bases well? What is it that makes the young player want to achieve excellence?

Children love to run. Even kids who run slowly love to run. Players who have little confidence catching, throwing or hitting will still rush to be first in line when it comes time to practice running the bases. For a lot of children, therefore, learning the fundamentals of base running is the gateway through which they will first build confidence in the game. A manager or coach has to encourage this skill, and they have to let the player know that he or she is good at it—whether or not they're fast or slow. Therefore, the very first thing to teach, and to praise, is the execution of proper base running. If certain players aren't very good yet at most other aspects of the sport, make them the ones to show the rest of the team how to run through first base on a grounder. Base running ought to be among the favorite parts of your practices because it can always be taught in a fun way. Even the weakest players can master it fairly quickly. Make the kids run, but while they're doing it start to teach them the subtleties of how to do it the right way. It's the foundational skill to turning on the younger or weaker players to baseball as a whole. Running is joy—let them express it on the base paths.

Throwing is the second most important skill to introduce to your weaker players because it's the next step in building their confidence. Some kids, for whatever reason, have a lot of trouble throwing a ball. Sometimes they release it too early or too late, but most often they tend to throw off the wrong foot. Still, beginning baseball players want to throw the ball, just like they want to run the bases. Maybe it's because they know they can't get hurt throwing, as opposed to having to catch or swing at an incoming ball, but a lot of kids are happy to fling it without the least bit of care about where it lands. More than most other baseball skills, throwing a ball is largely a physical concern. It's a matter of teaching children how to position their feet, how to shift their weight, what to do with their non-throwing glove hand, and how and when to release the ball. In order to be successful, your players need to at least learn how to reach the infield from the outfield, how to throw out runners at first and second base, and how to throw accurately across the diamond from third to first. Throwing takes practice; pitching, on the other hand, is far more a mental and emotional issue.

Because baseball is a game of failure, doom can enter at anytime. You can pitch brilliantly but then give up the one hit that loses the whole game. In a sense, what you have to teach your pitchers is not how to pitch well but how to pitch well after they fail. Young baseball players will often unravel after giving up a couple of walks or hits, let alone a couple of runs. They will lose all confidence. They will feel as if the eyes of the entire team, the coaches, their parents, and everyone else at the game are staring at them as things get worse and worse. Sometimes they will cry. And when they do, it's tempting to take them off the mound. But don't—at least not for that reason.

Your pitchers, of course, will tend to be the best players on your team. Although everyone has to learn how to throw well, only the kids with the strongest and most accurate arms will want to pitch. Pitching is very much a mental game. It's about poise, and to some extent it's about maintaining an angry, aggressive attitude. When your pitcher is on the mound you want him to know that he can get the batter out. More to the point, he himself has to be *convinced* that he will get the batter out. He is in control. Without this attitude, no pitcher—not one—will succeed in overcoming those moments when he or she will invariably fail.

Of course, there's also the physical aspects—the steps of the pitching motion, how to grip specific pitches, arm angles, how to field the position from the mound, how to determine what pitch to throw in a certain situation—but, more than anything, it's about attitude. Technique can be taught but success comes from within. A youth pitcher should be something like a pint-sized martial arts master. Only your most confident players should pitch. He or she has to keep his or her mind quiet, his or her thoughts controlled, and must learn to concentrate on only one thing: that batter is mine—he will fail, not me.

The hitter, of course, is thinking the same thing. This is his or her moment, one of only three or four times in the game where he or she is the focus of the offense. The batter has to have what might be described as a controlled ferocity. They want to pulverize the ball, but at the same time they have to stay disciplined and determined.

Hitting, while perhaps not as difficult as fielding, is a hard skill to teach to certain players. At first, some children will be afraid of getting hit by the ball. And with good reason—at some point, they will be hit by the ball. Whether that's because the opposing pitcher doesn't yet have good control, or because beginning hitters some-times crowd the plate, every batter *will* be hit somewhere on their body at some point. It may sting or even hurt for a while, but every child that's hit eventually gets up and makes his or her way to first base. It's a part of the game that all children have to deal with. And as they face that fear they learn the first lesson of successful hitting: don't be afraid of the ball.

One thing that's tough about teaching kids how to hit is that every child has something different to learn. Some need to learn how to properly grip the bat, or even which bat to select. Some have to learn where to stand in the batter's box, others how to plant their back foot, or how to shift their weight, or where to position their hands or their elbows. Some need to understand how to step into the pitch, how to keep their head still or how to simply get the timing down about when to swing. At first a lot of hitters even need to learn to drop the bat, rather than throwing it and potentially injuring someone.

Learning to catch a baseball likewise takes a bit of courage. In this respect, as with hitting, one of the first things you need to teach your players is to not be afraid of the ball. Even older kids, when they move up to higher levels of youth baseball, have to be reminded of this—especially when some of the more advanced players are suddenly throwing as fast as seventy miles per hour. Start the less experienced players slowly. Teach them to field ground balls first. Then move on to soft, underhand tosses from short distances and gradually lengthen those distances and start to throw it to them over-hand. They will likely, at some point, get hit in the face by the ball. They will cry. Then you will encourage them to get back in there and try to catch it again—and for sure, this next time, they'll be paying very close attention to the toss. A lot of players will stick their gloves out but shift their bodies away from a throw. Of course, you can't catch a ball consistently this way. You have to ease the kids into not being afraid by teaching them how to position the glove—sideways across your body if it's coming straight at you, tilted upward if it's above your waist, in the form of a basket if it's below your waist. You have to coax them into not swiping at the ball but rather allowing it to enter their gloves, and then demonstrate how to squeeze it and pull it to their bodies. Finally, and most importantly, you have to make sure your players follow the ball at all times. Younger children may be staring at the clouds or at their shoes, but as coach it's up to you to give them their first life lesson to always keep their eyes on the ball.

One drill that helps kids to overcome any fear they may have of the ball involves tossing a very soft ball, or a wiffle ball, high in the air and asking your players not to catch it but to bounce it off their heads. Kids—especially the soccer-playing ones—love this drill. It not only teaches them how to line up a fly ball but it shows them that the ball isn't especially life-threatening. It might sting, but then that little pinch of pain goes away.

Fielding the ball and playing a position correctly is, of course, related to catching, but rather than courage what the youth player needs most to excel is patience and the ability to listen and adjust. Actually, the coach needs a lot of patience too, because younger players get frustrated when they make fielding mistakes and older ones tend to think they know better. One of the cardinal rules to drill into your players is the importance of calling for the ball. A pop-up to the infield can be the cause of mass collisions among inexperienced players. And not just among the infielders—often a younger kid will race in from right field to make a play at the pitcher's mound. A team of young children will chase after a loose ball until it becomes a melee, grabbing the ball and running either around the bases with it or into the outfield. Some kids will push the base runner off the bag and then tag him, as if it's an out. It may not be harder to field than it is to hit, but it's definitely more difficult for the manager or coach to teach it to young children.

Teaching proper fielding technique—how to field grounders, how to block the ball with your body, where to be positioned, which base to throw to, how to hit the cut-off man, who covers second base—is the most difficult skills task the manager or coach has. Baseball games, at all levels, are won on defense—fielding and pitching. The best coaches will spend the lion's share of their practice time teaching fielding and throwing techniques.

How, then, do you encourage a kid lacking patience to concentrate and listen to instructions? There are two ways—you can threaten him by taking away playing time if he doesn't listen and berate him by explaining that his mistakes are hurting the team, or you can take the higher road. As for the latter, recommended direction, if you begin by inspiring your players in areas of the game in which they excel, then their confidence is greater in general. They'll want to play for you. And when they want to play—and play with confidence—you'll be amazed by how much their patience and concentration improves. Happy kids don't want to let their coaches down, and, more importantly, they don't want to let down their teammates or themselves. Confident baseball players play better because they listen and want to practice.

So, although this is a book about learning and teaching baseball skills, it's also about confidence, courage, patience, practice, discipline, concentration, and joy. It's really these intangible fundamentals that you have to successfully manage—both within yourself and your players—in order to forge a happy, winning baseball team.

Baseball is such an extraordinary game for children and adolescents because it combines graceful and energetic physical play with strategic, intellectual challenges. It's the perfect fire in which the courage of young people can be forged, because while an individual game may be the whole world to them at that moment, the actual result is relatively insignificant and largely forgotten over the long course of life. As for you, if they remember you at all, it will be for what kind of man or woman you were that season and not for the score of any game.

Your players do not have to reach the Little League World Series in Williamsport, Pennsylvania—now a nationally televised event!—to know that they're winners. Not that a first place finish isn't sweet or isn't the goal—it certainly is—but the surest path to victory lies in discovering and revealing the inner strengths within each boy and girl on your team.

DRAFTING YOUR PLAYERS (AND THEIR PARENTS)

At the very youngest age levels, most youth baseball leagues simply distribute all the registered players among the designated teams, and everyone happily goes off to play. A draft of players between the ages of five and either seven or eight really isn't necessary because most of them haven't yet developed adequate baseball skills. Moreover, the program for the very youngest players should always be focused on learning—and not particularly winning—the game. In fact, most T-ball teams (five and six year olds) don't even bother to keep score.

By age nine (or sometimes eight) youth baseball leagues will begin to hold drafts a couple of weeks before the season is set to start. Some coaches view the drafts as fun opportunities to get away for a couple of hours and have a beer or two with their peers. Others enjoy the thrill of taking fantasy baseball up a notch—you get to pick and choose real people! It's like playing with toy soldiers—except that they're alive! In reality, somewhat sadly, youth baseball drafts can devolve into shouting matches and name-calling, and coaches with bruised egos have been known to literally come to blows over the disposition of nine- and ten-year-olds. Such is the nature of parenthood—or in almost all cases, to be precise, fatherhood.

Coaches argue about anything. They argue over the rankings of players. They argue over the system of the draft—whether it should proceed from first to last pick, and then reverse; or whether a more scientific and completely incomprehensible approach, possibly first discovered in some of Einstein's unpublished papers, in which the person with the first overall pick drops to last in the second round, the person with the starting second pick then goes first . . . and et cetera, until mayhem ensues. At least everyone usually agrees that the original draft order should be picked out of a hat.

Typically, the league or division commissioner will prepare a list of all players that comprise the pool to be drafted. Kids will be ranked based on hitting, fielding and throwing abilities, and sometimes on base running as well. The rankings are determined either by coaches' comments from the previous year, or, particularly for the older players, tryouts that are held prior to the start of the season.

When your turn to pick comes around you naturally will want to pick the best player available. You can perhaps gauge who's best based on where he or she's ranked—but year-old rankings aren't especially reliable with respect to developing children, and coaches who want to "protect" their favorite players for later rounds sometimes give notoriously inaccurate ratings to otherwise excellent players. Alternatively, you can ask your fellow coaches to identify the best remaining player on the board. But more often than not they won't tell you the truth.

Is youth baseball really so cutthroat? Yes, it can be. Not among the players, of course, but among the coaches it can be ruthless.

In any event, you have to pick someone, so what are the criteria to rely on? Most games are won on pitching and defense. Therefore, if your choice is between a kid who catches and throws very well and a player who hits well, always take the better pitcher and fielder. A nine- or ten-year-old team that plays excellent defense is at a huge advantage over its opponents. In particular, when selecting your team, pitching always trumps batting.

At the tryouts, if your league holds them, pay very close attention to how each player hits, throws, and fields. You often won't get a long look, because there are a lot of kids to see in a limited amount of time, so focus on a batter's form rather than how far he hits; on a fielder's grace when moving to pick up grounders or lining up fly balls rather than whether or not she catches one; and on the strength and ease of delivery when throwing rather than whether the player was accurate. Make your own notes for each player, and find the time to re-rank the players based on what you've observed.

A lot of baseball players in all youth leagues have been players from a young age—as early as four or five years old. A standout at age six is not necessarily a top player by age ten. But this same player, who's been around the league for four years, has a reputation among coaches and parents as an excellent player based on the impressions formed at a very young age. That player will be ranked high, accordingly, even though his or her skill level may not be as advanced as other, less-well-known players. There are a lot of overrated players in youth baseball, but a lot of underrated ones as well. Your task, especially as a new coach at a draft, is to uncover the hidden gems.

So once you've attended the tryouts, made diligent notes, created your own ranking system, and retrieved as much intelligence as you can from the competing coaches—you're still not done. One remaining factor, and arguably the most important factor, is to learn about the parents of the kids you want to draft. In other words, you have to understand how to draft your parents.

If the first radical concept discussed here addresses the commitment a successful coach should have to the players at the bottom of his order, the second is that your job, as a volunteer coach, includes serving the parents of your players. Not at the pizza place during your end-of-season party, but throughout your schedule of games.

This might be a shocking concept to a lot of grizzled old youth baseball coaches, but these parents, second only to your players, are a primary audience for you. Think about it: most parents attend the games, they likely practice baseball at least once in a while with their kids, they keenly know how vital baseball is to their sons and daughters, and—in that context—they are placing their children in your hands for at least a few very important hours each week. Appreciate these people and be responsive to them right from the start. A happy coach needs happy parents.

The majority of parents want to be involved in youth baseball because their kids genuinely enjoy playing, or otherwise like the game and want to learn how to play. They may or may not practice regularly with their son or daughter, and they may or may not have had any baseball experience in their youth. But this very large category of parents generally wants their children to have fun—not to receive major league baseball training, not to win at all costs—but simply to have fun.

A smaller group of parents have their kids get involved because they believe, rightly or wrongly, that their children are baseball prodigies. These parents agitate for more practices, simultaneous participation in more than one baseball league, professional training, a win-at-all-costs coaching regimen and an insistence that their little stars be at the center of each game. Often these kids are very good players—but their inclusion on a team can cause difficulties for a coach. Parents like these tend to stand on the sidelines and criticize not only the coaches but, amazingly, even the poor play of kids other than their own.

If you're the type of coach that's in it just to win it, then this somewhat coddled prodigy-child is right for you. If, however, you're the sort of coach that recognizes that the importance of winning must be balanced with creating opportunities for young people to grow, you'll do far better with players who also have well-behaved parents.

A baseball season can be difficult. Sometimes kids don't play well, or, more often, don't play as well as they expect themselves to play, and they easily lose confidence. Invariably, at some point in the season, the team itself seems to slip into a rut, usually due to sudden poor hitting or fielding. And even when things are going well—even if your team hasn't lost a game all season—you have to guard against complacency and recognize that it's especially then that all the other coaches will want to beat you and your players.

So, when you draft a team, you need to not only try to pick players who are good pitchers and fielders but also those, to the extent possible, with cool parents around whom you can build a winning team spirit.

How in the world do you do this? There's no tryout for parents. Well, depending on the community you live in, and the length of time you've been involved with your respective youth baseball league, it shouldn't be as hard as it might sound. Pick your own son's or daughter's friends—there's a good chance you already know something about their parents. Pick kids your child might know from school—in fact, ask your own kid prior to the draft whether or not he or she knows certain other children. Finally, choose players with parents who you already know because they may very well be the ones available to help you as assistant coaches.

So, to recap, draft your players in this order:

- Good pitchers
- Good fielders
- Good hitters
- Fast runners
- Kids with cool parents
- And, across the board, players around whom you can build a winning team spirit

Once your players are selected, there are several ways to start building such a team. First, although it should be self-evident, be certain to always treat each of your players equally. That doesn't mean that every player gets equal time at their favorite positions, regardless of playing ability, but it does mean that every player is equally worthy of your effort and attention. It's extremely tempting to favor your best players and want to work with them the most. In fact, there may very well be children on your team that will never learn to play the game successfully. But it is a huge mistake to distance yourself from, or in any way marginalize, these players and their parents. If you take the time to teach the game to your worst players, you will end up with a motivated and ultimately successful bottom of your batting order. Giving time and attention to your least able players is not only rewarding in itself, not only a big factor in creating happy players (and parents) and a winning team spirit, but it's also a cold-blooded advantage over competitive teams. Every team will have some talented players. But the kids with the least talent on all the teams will also get plenty of at-bats—be the coach that makes those at-bats most effective.

Second in importance to building team spirit is good communications, both with your players and your players' parents. Let each player know what expectations you have for them. If they want to pitch, make sure they know that they have to be ready; and, if they're not yet ready, make sure they know that they have to show you more at practice before you put them in the game. The same holds true for any field position.

How you structure your batting order is up to you, and there are specific guidelines offered in Chapter 6, but in any event, be certain that your players know why they are slotted into specific batting order levels (if you do so) and what they need to do to move up in the batting order (if you allow that to be possible).

Third, try never to yell at or berate your players. It may be okay to shout at a player who is not giving his or her full effort in an attempt to wake them up, but it's not okay to shout at a child who makes an error or, worst of all, because you're frustrated about their play on the field. Under no circumstances should a coach take out his or her anger on any player—even if that player is your own child. Coaches who loudly chastise, or even humiliate, their own children, thinking that it's okay because, after all, it's their kid, not only stigmatize that player in front of his or her peers and embarrass themselves but they also embarrass everyone else watching—including the rest of the team.

As a rule, never, ever, ever humiliate a player by berating them in front of their peers.

At the end of a losing game, during your team meeting, find the positive things that happened on the field and open your remarks by praising those good plays. As players get older, they can take harsher criticism, but in general make the game fun for your team whether you win or lose. Don't let children go home feeling small because they made a bad play or simply because the team lost.

The fourth, and perhaps most important element, of building a winning team spirit is humor. Baseball is a game—have fun doing it. Use humor to keep your players loose, and use it to subtly communicate to them that the baseball field is a place to have fun. It's not school. It's not the military. And for virtually everyone who plays, except for those who ultimately turn professional, it's not even real life. Try to make your kids laugh.

Try to make your parents laugh, too. A lot of successful coaches, particularly of younger children, like to send out game summaries to all the parents after every win or loss. These summaries ideally should highlight some of the better plays of the game, and, where possible, point out excellent plays made by every member on the team. Parents love to see their own kids' names up in lights, so to speak. And if these game summaries are humorous, all the better. Here's an amusing one received from my son's coach after a needlessly argumentative game in which the opposing coach apparently forgot that his baseball team was comprised of eight-year-olds:

> Dear Team . . . We trust all of our fantastic moms of our fabulous **BRAVES** had a wonderful Mother's Day weekend! For

those of you who may have missed the game Saturday, it was a doozy, a passionate, come-from-behind, 14-7 win over the Red Sox! Our fighting **BRAVES**, down to only eight regular players and one special guest call-up from the 7s Division, got off to a slow start, and after two innings we fell behind 6-0, due, in part, to a grand slam home run by one of the opposing players. But to be a **BRAVE**, of course, means to never give up. We scratched out two runs in the bottom of the third, and then tied the game 6-6 in the bottom of the fourth, thanks to some timely hitting by old friend **Andrew**, our 7s guest star, dressed sharply for the occasion in his retro 2009 Angels jersey; **Josh**, who was saving his best hitting for later; **Harry**, who ended up going five-for-five in the game; and clean-up hitter **Jon**, who finished with 3 RBIs. But the Red Sox came back with a run in the bottom of the fourth to take a 7-6 lead. Meanwhile, we got some clutch pitching from **Harry**, who tossed a scoreless third, and **Jon**, who took the mound in relief in the fourth inning with no outs and the bases loaded to strike out the side. Then, in the top of the fifth, our **BRAVES** really started to groove. After base hits by **Julie** and **Andrew**, **Josh, a.k.a the "Babe,"** came to the plate. Some say he pointed to the center-field fence on his way to the box, and perhaps he did, because he then launched a mammoth shot in that direction for a three-run homer and a 9-7 **BRAVES** lead! After that, the umpire and coaches from both teams convened near the pitching mound to exchange pleasantries and offer thoughtful opinions about league rules. After a few air kisses, and, in a classy touch, a presentation by **Coach Ryan** of a lovely bouquet of orchids and a box of chocolates to the opposing head coach, the game resumed. With the Red Sox batting, and a man on first, their batter produced a scorching line drive which appeared to head into leftfield. However, **Harry, a.k.a "Derek Jeter circa**

1998," leaped into the air, snatched the blazing ball, rifled it to first base and picked off the runner for a double-play. And then, in the top of the sixth, tying a record set by the 1937 St. Louis Browns, the **BRAVES** put the game away with nine straight singles from **Lawrence, Julie, Andrew, Josh, Brian** (who missed a home run over the left-field fence by three inches), **Kevin, Harry, Jon,** and **Alex** for the 14-7 victory. After the game, the team medic provided **Coach Ryan** with several nitroglycerin pills.

Of course, that's not exactly what happened. There was actually a huge argument about rules between the head coaches, and a lot of regrettable yelling and shouting, but the humor contained in the game report made a lot of the parents laugh and helped to endear them to the coach. The fact that the coach noticed—and reported— at least one accomplishment by each of the players further helped the parents to feel that their sons and daughters were being treated with respect. This particular team, incidentally, went on to finish in first place that year.

Now, you're not always going to have a successful draft. The kid you thought would pitch well might not be as good as advertised. At times, your better players might get injured, or might be away, or might be punished by their parents for bad behavior and be forced to miss games. It's also not so easy to build team spirit when you do end up with a spoiled kid, or a baseball prima donna, on the field.

Every once in awhile this type of kid pops up on your team. This is the sort of player who is in it for himself, who is likely immature and who shows little feelings for the other kids on the team. He wants—and will demand—attention, praise and applause. He may be a talented baseball player, but he is a lot of times also a bully. You have to be assertive with this sort of a player, but you also have to understand that it's not your job to change him—even though he, too, deserves your full consideration and attention. Indeed, with the right approach, you can encourage this kid to be a team player and give him a different kind of self-confidence that, for all his bravado, he lacks.

You often can't compromise with a kid like this, or with his parents. Nor should you. Really the best, and perhaps the only, successful way to deal with him is to let him do what he wants on the field—at first. The coach unquestionably must protect his or her other players from any abuse, but he also has the keep the team united, with or without the support of a difficult kid. And, of course, the coach—the adult on the field—must at all times be assertive.

As long as you're in control, these sorts of kids won't push you around. They will attempt, however, to boss around the other players. There are three keys to dealing with prima donna baseball players, and the first one is to test his character.

This is the kind of kid who wants the ball, so give him the ball. Put him in the most challenging situations on the field, where the game is on the line. Prima donnas believe they will succeed, because they have in the past, so you naturally want your best player at the fulcrum of every turning point of the game. Using him in this way stokes the always-burning embers of his ego. It keeps him happy, and it keeps his parents happy. More to the point, it also sets him up to eventually fail—and that's a good thing. Not every kid, no matter how good, is going to make every pitch, get every hit and snag every important catch. The prima donna will naturally look, at first, to blame someone else for his failure, but deep inside that poor performance will take the kid down a notch. At the right time, a coach can subtly remind the prima donna that he, too, sometimes fails. This failure, and the knowledge of such failure, is actually a step toward building good character. Further, it draws the player, in his own mind, closer to the human level of his peers on the team.

Second, give him a leadership role. A lot of these children may be star athletes, but they're challenged when given responsibility for other players. Allow the prima donna to lead certain parts of the practice, for example, infield drills or base-running exercises. Put him in a leadership position, with close supervision, and see if the kid actually sinks or swims. Again, if he succeeds, then you're closer to building a more cohesive team. And if he fails, then you've given him an opportunity to polish his character.

The third element to dealing with the prima donna is to expose him to the other players. Children are smart, and they are keenly perceptive about how other children behave among their peers. If you emphasize the role of the prima donna player, and you give him increasing responsibility, it's more likely than not that he will eventually fall flat on his face. That experience not only tempers his ego, but it provides a rallying point for the other players—they feel less threatened by him when they see him fail, and they, in turn, will appreciate the opportunity to encourage him. In fact, it's often the least capable players who will reach out to encourage the star prima donna to move on. This is another example of why the so-called worst players on your team are essential to a team's success.

So, consider again how to draft the least talented players on your team. Presuming that at the end of the draft you're left with a pool of players that don't particularly throw, bat or field well, how do you select one over another? Simply look for the ones that you think have any of these attributes:

- Cool parents
- Strong character
- At least one potential skill strength: either batting, fielding, or throwing
- Equipped at the tryout with major league baseball team apparel.

Okay, so the last point is an important criterion only if you're completely stuck. But note the kids who come to the tryouts wearing the caps of their favorite teams or the jerseys of their favorite players. You'll know, at least, that they love the game. And that's more than enough to work with.

3

RUNNING YOUR PRACTICES

One of the first orders of business at the time of your initial team practice is to establish respect from your players. Neither children nor adults will work hard for a leader that they don't respect.

Respect is relatively easy to achieve if you already have an extensive baseball background, or, in the case of coaching youth baseball, you're an obvious athlete in your early twenties. But for the rest of us who may no longer technically be in our athletic prime, there are a few useful tools that set the stage for effective leadership.

The first of these is listening. Yes, you first have to listen to your players and their parents—not the other way around. So many parents, particularly of younger aged children, are eager to give their kids' new coach early scouting reports. Further, these opening comments aren't limited to how good their own boy or girl is but, more often than not, they concern how inexperienced their player might be. Sometimes a parent wants to share with the coach about certain health issues. Sometimes there's a concern that the child had a poor experience playing last season, or that he or she doesn't really want to be there, or that there's a conflict sometimes with soccer practice (that's a big one), or that the kid has his own catcher's equipment—so that's where he's expected to play.

Also explain to parents at this first practice that the playing time during the games will often be dominated by those players who most often come to practice.

Just as importantly, or maybe more importantly, listen to your players at the first practice. A lot of them might be shy, so you need to draw them out. Try to find out what they think are their strengths. Find out where they like to play. Especially find out if any of them have experience, or even an interest, in pitching. Try to determine who are friends with whom on the team, where they go to school, and eventually what their likes and dislikes might be. Which is their favorite professional baseball team? Favorite player? You'll need to understand what makes each kid tick in order to motivate and challenge them later in the season. The key to having fun—and winning—is to listen.

A second important factor to establishing respect is discipline. You have to be serious about discipline or you will eventually lose your team. They're kids, of course, so they will appear to behave as if they always listen to you. But if they don't respect you, they won't hear you, and you'll have trouble motivating them after that.

Practices should start with running. And you, as coach, ideally should do it with them. When running laps, stay in a single-file line and do not allow talking. If anyone tries to cut corners, make them stop to do push-ups. If a player continues to cut corners, make the entire team stop to do push-ups. If that doesn't work, have them run extra laps. Before you even take the field, you have to figure out how to make the kids behave and want to pay attention to you. As a coach, you're there to teach them how to play baseball and, if you're lucky, maybe teach them a thing or two about overcoming obstacles in life. But you're not there to screw around.

After at least five minutes of running, take about ten to fifteen minutes for stretching exercises. Stretching is a good icebreaker, a good opportunity to get to know your players. Learn their names. Start to figure out who likes to play where. Try to determine how long they've played baseball. And introduce your assistant coaches.

It's important to develop assistant coaches who will make themselves available to the team on both practice and game days. The coaches are almost always mothers or fathers of the kids on your team, but you can always reach out to friends and co-workers as well. (In most leagues, assistant coaches, like coaches, will of course have to submit to background checks.) Your assistants will help run different stations during your practice drills and typically also serve as base coaches on game days. You'll also want an assistant to tally the scorecard during your games so that you have accurate reports of each player's progress. Ideally, you want coaches who know something about baseball or at least sports in general. But far more importantly, you need assistants who will be available and not leave you alone with the team to run everything by yourself.

It's essential to have a plan in mind before each practice—do you need to work on hitting, fielding, pitching, or base running? If so, which drills will you emphasize throughout the practice, and how many minutes do you plan to devote to each drill? It's vital to stay on the clock to be sure that everything is accomplished in the limited time available. Make sure your assistant coaches know the particular practice plan as well.

A very effective practice can be structured within ninety minutes—this would include running, stretching, fielding, batting, and base running drills. A two-hour practice is ideal, but kids are busy and field space is limited, so you may not have the luxury of either time or practice space.

It's especially difficult to have enough room, or even baseball field availability, to run an efficient practice in an urban area. There's limited space and too many teams, not to mention competition from other sports leagues, such as soccer and football. With this in mind, if you are an urban youth baseball coach (or if you're alone without an assistant coach to help), adjust your practices to best accommodate your team and its space considerations. As with everything, make do with what you've got. As long as there's a ball and a patch of dirt or asphalt, your players will want to practice. The key is to always try to have everyone busy doing something. If you don't have the ability to have more than one drill happening at the same time, then utilize drills that necessarily involve pairs of players—two-player groups practicing soft-toss batting, pitchers paired with catchers, or infield ground ball drills.

However, if you do have access to a field, begin your practice by setting up stations. These stations consist of concentrated practice areas—for example, a throwing station, or a groundball-fielding station—during which you and your assistant coaches can offer individual drills and coaching to perhaps four or fewer members of your team. Generally, try to start the kids at the stations where they're strongest, and then shift them to their weaker stations. Again, at each moment you have to be conscious of how you can help all the children on your team to build confidence. Everyone wants to start with the exercise that they perform best.

In youth baseball, especially below the age of twelve, the players really should be learning to play every position. As early as the ages of seven or eight, of course, you can tell pretty fast who has the ability to play infield best and who might otherwise be tucked away in right field. However, you're doing not only a disservice to your team but a great disservice to the individual player if you don't expose each child to each position—especially at a young age—and teach them how to play those respective positions.

Every child on your team under the age of nine should be given an opportunity sometime during the season to play all the field positions, or especially whichever position he or she desires, with the possible exceptions of first base and pitcher. The problem with first base is that certain kids playing the infield will whip the ball to first for a play, and a child who doesn't catch well can be hurt. And the challenge of pitching at this age, of course, is that certain children can't throw well enough yet to reach home plate, let alone pitch strikes. Others may be scared to death just at the thought of taking the ball.

As your players get older, the positions become more set. Players of relatively limited ability under the age of eleven, for example, should still be given opportunities to play the infield but they will also spend more of their time in the outfield as the quality of play becomes more competitive and your best fielders end up playing the infield on a regular basis. By the time kids are twelve years old, regular positions on a youth baseball team will largely be set.

Most of your practice stations will concern either fielding or hitting. Base running, of course, is crucial, but that is best drilled with the entire team together. And pitching will typically involve only certain players. Pitching drills should be split off from the rest of the team or, even better, held together with your catchers at a separate time from your full team practice.

For a twelve-player team, it's most effective to run three different stations during your practices. For one thing, if you're lucky, you'll likely have no more than two other assistant coaches to help. Secondly, groups of four or less work best because there's more of an individual feel and less screwing around by your players as compared to when you might have them in a larger group. There are any number of drills that can be performed, and many will be described throughout this book, but for the purpose of this demonstration, let's set up three basic fielding stations.

These three basic stations will invariably include groundball fielding, outfield practice and throwing. In other words, a third of the team will be in the infield learning/practicing how to field grounders; a third will be in the outfield learning/practicing how to catch fly balls; and a third will be off to one side working on their throwing techniques. This is the place and the time to fix what's wrong. Once you identify a problem area—their ready positions, perhaps, or how they're failing to properly line up a fly ball—approach the individual player and crouch down so that you're speaking to them eye-to-eye. Through this approach, children feel less criticized by an authority figure but more encouraged by someone they perceive to be caring and equal.

Each player should spend at least ten minutes (or more) at each station. When the time is up, the groups rotate. Accordingly, you'll end up spending at least thirty minutes on fielding drills over the course of a ninety-minute practice. Together with your twenty minutes of running and stretching, you're now fifty minutes into your practice.

Hitting stations should follow next. Again, set up your three stations with you and your assistant coaches manning each of the three areas. Typical hitting stations will include batting off of a tee, hitting soft tosses, and facing live pitching. Each of these drills, as well as others, are described in detail in Chapter 12. For the purpose of this exercise, however, you'll again rotate your team every ten minutes through these stations for a total of thirty minutes. You now are eighty minutes into your practice—leaving you ten minutes for base running and words of encouragement before your break. Of course, if you have two hours or more set aside for practice, the length of time at each station can be accordingly lengthened. The key, no matter how long of a practice session you have, is to keep every player occupied at all times. As soon as a kid starts standing around, you lose him.

As you establish respect from your team by listening and through discipline, you will invariably also have to deal with when and how to punish "poor" behavior by a player. Such behavior could include laziness, belligerence, or even the teasing or bullying of teammates. It's usually no more than a kid not wanting to run or not making his best efforts during an exercise. A baseball team isn't a military platoon, and you're dealing with sensitive children, not grown men and women, so as a general rule be lenient. But when the behavior starts to affect the morale of the team, or interferes with what you're trying to accomplish, then the coach has to step in. It's not necessarily effective to correct that player by having him or her sit out, or by doing push-ups while everyone else watches and waits. Rather, set forth a rule that laziness or other poor behavior will be punished by making the entire team do extra running or suicide drills. This latter drill consists of having the team run at full speed from the first-base line to the base path between second and third; then, at the coach's command, suddenly reverse; then suddenly reverse direction again, until everyone is exhausted. Kids hate this drill. Punishing the entire team reinforces the idea that teammates have to be responsible for each other's acts. Most imma-ture kids sober up quickly when they see their peers suffering as a result of their individual behaviors.

Although some coaches shout at their players mercilessly, that's not an ideal way to either motivate or punish kids. Most children will withdraw when they're yelled at, internalize the criticism and feel terribly about themselves. This is the opposite of joy, and it's not what you want to see in a youth baseball team. Never shout at a player out of your own anger or frustration. Yell at them to wake them up when they're spaced out in the field. Shout at them when they're on the bench and despondent because they think they're going to lose the game. And, in the rare case of an extremely boneheaded play, never isolate or vilify the player that blew the play—punish the entire team by making all of them run.

At the end of practice, get the team together and speak to them eye-to-eye. If you have them kneel, then you take a knee too. If they're standing in a group, crouch down to their level. You never want to set yourself apart, above your players. Rather, always be one of them, to the extent possible. If they have a question about a play or a technique, don't just tell them but pick up a bat and show them. Baseball is a game of skill, and of strategy, but it's also a game of intense psychology. At your end-of-practice meeting, make sure you go over the skills you observed that need to be improved, but always close the practice with praise and encouragement.

At each subsequent practice, consider reducing the number of push-ups to be done, or the amount of laps run. This subtly communicates to your players that they're getting better as the season progresses.

You want your players to love to play, and, in particular, to love to play for you. Leave them excited about the job they did at the end of the day, and inspire them to want to come back to the field again and again.

4

HOW TO RUN THE BASES LIKE A PRO

You would think that running to first base should be an easy task, but for most young players even this skill needs to be taught. Children, first, must be trained over and over to not look at the ball after they hit it and when they run. It's a very bad baseball habit that some kids have great difficulty breaking. A lot of young players even stand in the batter's box after they hit the ball, either admiring what they've just done or maybe shocked that they did it. Often the first base coach has to shout at them to run! Batters who constantly look at the ball as they run down to first base will lose the precious seconds that often determine whether they'll be safe or out. Make sure, from Day One, that your players don't do this.

As players get older and more experienced, however, it's advisable for them to learn to take a very quick glance at the fielders when they're perhaps four to five steps out of the box to see how the play is progressing and whether an error has been made that might entitle them to take second. Additionally, your players at every age should learn to take a quick glance over their right shoulder immediately *after* they cross first base in case an overthrow or an error might allow them to continue on to second.

The first-base coach is responsible for reinforcing these techniques during games at least through the age of eight. He should be loud and demonstrative on every play, spurring the batter out of the box, hustling her down the line even if it looks like a sure out and reminding her not to look at the ball. Of course, that coach also has to direct the young player to run to second if there's a chance for two and remind the player, once she's on base, of the various and varied things that might happen on the next play which she has to keep in mind. As players get older and more experienced on the base paths, they appropriately learn to run more aggressively. Accordingly, in the older divisions, the first-base coach generally needs to be little more than a stop sign. By then, players better know to focus on running through the bag and not gaze at the ball as they make their way down the base path.

After the player puts the ball in play with a hit, they need to learn how to drop—not throw—the bat and quickly spring out of the batter's box. The first step out of the box should be with the runner's

| *Correctly not looking at the ball* | *Incorrectly looking at the ball* |

Running through first base.

back foot. She should pump her arms straight back, run on her toes, and dash in a straight line to first. Moreover, the runner must engage in a full-out sprint right down the base path and *through* first base. He or she isn't running to the base, but instead must go past it. A lot of younger players not used to this concept will often stop right on the bag, sometimes slide, and sometimes even dive headfirst. But the fastest way to be safe is to run right through that base. Coaches need to drill this skill with their new teams preferably as early as the first practice.

As the runner approaches the base, ideally she wants to touch the front of the bag, the edge that's closest to her as she runs. In the meantime, she ought to lean slightly forward, like a racer at the finish line, and then take small stutter steps once she passes the base in order to slow down as quickly as possible and to not run too far down the right field line. But she should certainly not slow down before she reaches the base. This sounds obvious, but a lot of young players will start to hit the brakes just as they approach the bag. Whether or not this slight deceleration results in an actual out, it certainly helps to create an impression, for the umpire, that the runner indeed was out.

Once the runner successfully reaches first, he or she—after passing through the bag—generally ought to turn right, into foul territory, to make his or her way back to the base. If the runner turns to the left, back onto the field, and then demonstrates to the umpire what he perceives as an intent to move on to second base, she can

Turning into foul territory.

be thrown out or tagged by the first baseman before returning to the base.

Hitting the brakes with a stutter step, after passing the bag, is useful, because if the throw gets away from the first baseman, then the runner is in relatively good position to take second base on the error. On the contrary, if the runner has proceeded too far down the right field line, spacing out and waving hello to the opposing right fielder, then he or she will be unlikely to cover that distance if the errant ball is still playable.

If the first base coach or the runner sees that the just-hit ball reaches the outfield in fair territory, then the runner should at least take a turn at first and proceed in the direction of second base. If the ball was fielded cleanly by the outfielder and thrown back in, then the runner must stop right away and head back to first.

On a deeper hit, or where the outfielder has difficulty picking up the ball, the runner should prepare to turn the hit into at least a double. Accordingly, as early as possible in the run to first, that batter should proceed outside of the base path, and blaze a wider arch in her first-base approach.

As the runner approaches first with an aim of taking second, she should target the front, inside corner of the bag, preferably touch it with her right foot, and be in a position with her body square to second. By proceeding in this fashion, the runner should, after passing first, be in a perfect place to run to second in a straight line. At the very least, the runner ought to make an aggressive turn at first base. If she sees that the outfielder already has possession of the ball, she generally should turn back to the first. But if the outfielder

Run on extra base hit.

has bobbled it, or perhaps thrown it past the cut-off man, or if neither the shortstop nor the second baseman is covering second, then she should aggressively attempt to turn her hit into a double.

Aggressive base running—as opposed to stupid base running—should be praised and encouraged, especially at the younger levels, and without regard to whether the runner was thrown out. Aggressive base running means the player had a chance to make it; stupid base running means it was a snowball's chance in hell.

If the runner indeed returns to first base, however, he has to be careful to pay attention to what's happening on the field. A nonchalant runner, strolling back to first base with his back to the field of play, can be picked off before he gets to the bag. While the ball is live, everyone on the field—base runners and defensive players—must be alert.

Younger players especially need to be drilled in certain basic base running rules that older players take for granted but which nevertheless often cause arguments between coaches, controversial calls by umpires, and sometimes the loss of a game.

Among these basic rules, coaches should train their players to touch every base while running. It's surprising how often youth baseball players miss a base. Home runs can be challenged and taken away, and doubles will turn into outs if an alert catcher or first baseman notices that the runner missed a bag. During your base running drills at practice, have the entire team at the very least run around the bases several times. As the season progresses, if kids still are missing the base during these drills, require everyone to run outfield laps. It's a basic skill to touch every base, but it's vitally important. If you're going to lose a game, don't lose because of such negligent base running.

A second obvious rule to make sure your base runners understand is to not run with abandon on pop-ups or fly balls if there are less than two outs. If a player takes off on such hits, that player will almost certainly be doubled off once the catch is made. On a deeper outfield hit, for sure, players should be encouraged to take a healthy lead in case the ball isn't fielded. But at the younger age divisions, where infield pop-ups are more prevalent, the kids have to be trained not to stray too far on such hits.

Of course, it often happens at the younger age levels that an infielder will miss the pop-up but still have time to recover, pick up the ball, and throw the runner holding up at first out at second, but that's youth baseball. It's more important for training, and to prepare for play at later levels, to be sure that your runners do not advance on what will be routine double plays as they get older.

One of the challenges in teaching younger players not to advance on fly balls is that, at first, they are nervous about base running. When there's an important play in the field, everyone is yelling what to do, but the young player hears nothing but white noise. His heart is in his throat. To overcome this tendency, and to enable your players to run the bases instinctively, you have to train them in practice through the implementation of different base running scenarios: runner at first, one out; runner at second with no one at first and one out; first and third, etc. Sometimes hit fly balls in those situations, sometimes grounders. These repetitive situational base running drills will implant deep in your player's subconscious the different possible permutations of base running that he'll face in a game. As a result, before the end of the season, your now-masterful base runners should respond coolly when the crucial moments come.

Back to the runner at first: once he's safe, and the next hitter prepares to bat, the runner has to get ready to advance on a subsequent play. For younger age groups (generally eight years old or below), stealing and taking leads are not allowed. Still, there are certain base running imperatives to follow when these younger players are on base. When holding on first, they should take a position with their left foot at the side of the bag, on their toes and not their heels, and facing the batter.

A lot of kids, instead, think it's advantageous to be in a crouch facing second base, as if in a runner's starting block, but such a position prevents the runner from having a clear view of the pitcher and especially the batter. Similarly, when on second base, the left foot

Foot position on first base.

again is against the side of the bag, arms relaxed, and the runner is on his toes facing first base. On third, the runner again should have his left foot at the edge of the bag, on his toes, and facing second base, or more precisely, the interior of the infield. Positioned in this way, runners always have a full view of the upcoming play.

Taking a Lead

If leads are allowed in your league, then coach your players to take a few shuffle steps off the base—without crossing their feet, be on their toes, or on the balls of their feet, with arms relaxed in front and to not lean toward the next base in case they have to quickly return to the bag on a pick-off attempt.

Players need to individually gauge the right distance for them to take a lead: it has to be far enough to give an advantage toward second, but close enough to allow them to get back to first on all but the most perfect pickoff attempt. They should also be focused on signs from the coaches—whether or not to steal can be either up to

Taking a lead

the coach, or, in some cases, at the runner's discretion, depending on the player's capability and baseball IQ.

At all times, the runner, especially if he's taking a lead, has to be aware of where the baseball is and, at most times, what the pitcher is doing. For example, a runner may break from third to steal home if he sees that the pitcher has received the ball from the catcher well in front of the mound and, with his back turned to the plate, is casually making his way back to the rubber without paying any attention to that runner on third. A player taking a lead especially has to be on notice that he can be picked off at anytime by either the pitcher or the catcher. If the pitcher is right-handed, the runner should especially watch the pitcher's right heel. That pitcher can't pickoff anyone at first unless he lifts that heel or steps back. Another hint is to watch that right-handed pitcher's glove-hand shoulder. That shoulder has to open toward first base on a pickoff attempt but stay closed on a pitch home.

Stealing on lefties is even more difficult. Generally, train your players not to break until they're sure that the pitcher's going home with the throw. Watch that southpaw pitcher for either a step back or a step toward the first baseline. Some lefties also tend to hold their hands either higher or lower than usual just prior to a pickoff move.

Generally, don't encourage your runners with leads to further advance on a line drive or shallow pop-up. Instead, drill them to stay very close to the bag. If your runner is on second base, he typically can take a longer lead because the middle infielders are much less likely to hold him on.

STEALING

Whether your runner is younger or older, less or more experienced, you as a coach should also drill them in how to break for the next base either on a hit or on a steal. To maximize acceleration, a runner should start low, as if in an abbreviated crouch, and then rise into a more normal running position once she gains velocity.

Springing out of a crouch.

When attempting a steal, it's important for older players to take the same lead, and act in the same way as they had on previous pitches. If they tip themselves off to the opposing catcher by, for example, taking a larger-than-normal lead or leaning more toward second, they give the other team the advantage to either throw them out or pick them off.

Stealing third base in some ways is easier than swiping second. Particularly when a right-handed batter is at the plate, that batter can serve as an extra obstacle for the catcher to make a clean throw. Additionally, runners on second are rarely held on by the shortstop or second baseman as compared to the first baseman's defensive position with a runner on. And left-handed pitchers particularly have difficulty picking off runners on second because they have to turn just about completely around to make an accurate throw.

One heads-up play that occasionally produces great results is a steal immediately after a walk. A lot of times the team in the field will relax or exhale a little too much after a walk—the pitch may be poorly thrown back to the mound, the pitcher may be looking up at the sky or emotionally distracted, and the batter who just walked, if he hustled down to first, can sometimes just keep on going to second base. By the time the defense realizes what happened, he may already be standing on second.

The steal of second on a walk is particularly effective when there's a base runner on third. If the pitcher or catcher attempts to throw out the runner at second, the man on third will almost always come home to score on the play. My son's ten-year-old team once even won a game in the bottom of the sixth inning on a walk-off walk: the batter earned a base on balls, attempted to steal second and ended up coming all the way home after a series of overthrows and errors. The potential to steal after a base on balls is just one reason why your players should be encouraged to always hustle down to first base on a walk.

Nevertheless, in recreational leagues, runners are stealing on catchers a lot more than they're stealing on pitchers. It's advisable to generally instruct your players to wait for the pitched ball to evade the catcher before taking an extra base, especially third base—unless that right-handed batter gets in the way, catchers typically prefer throwing down to third because the distance from home to third is considerably shorter than that from home to second. At least according to the Pythagorean Theorem, it should be.

Runners on Second Base

An important base running note applies to runners on second when there's no runner on first. Quite apart from the rules pertaining to runners dealing with fly balls and less than two outs, coaches also should train their players how or whether or not to advance from second on ground balls. Generally, when a ball is hit on the ground to the right side of the infield, behind the runner (e.g. first or second base), the runner on second should always advance to third.

It's a bit more challenging, however, when the grounder is to the left side (third base or shortstop). Generally in such a situation, the runner on second should stay relatively close to the bag. The fielder, if he fields the ball cleanly, typically will look the runner back to the base and then throw to get the batter at first. Once the throw is released, though, that runner on second—if he's alert and relatively fast—can take off for third. At the younger age levels, that runner will almost always be safe—to say the least, it's difficult for a first baseman under nine years old to rifle the ball back to his third-grader third baseman for a tag play. As kids get older, though, that advance becomes more difficult. At older levels, and with more capable players, that runner on second should only advance on a similar play if the corner infielders are relatively weak or if your runner is particularly fast.

Sliding

Whether stealing or simply advancing on a hit, runners will often have to slide—one of the more fun and exciting parts of the game.

Coaches absolutely have to teach their players how to slide. It's not only a vital skill determining whether your runner will be safe or out, but an incorrect or awkward slide can definitely cause injury. For youth recreational leagues, headfirst slides are typically not allowed. This is because a headfirst slide can be the cause of a host of injuries, ranging from jammed thumbs to concussions. Feet-first slides, when done the right way, are much safer for kids and very effective. Every kid loves to slide. Who doesn't want to get their uniform dirty?

There are a few easy steps to teach a child how to slide. First, when approaching the base, the player's arms should rise into the air as they also start to lean back. Second, the player will raise, or slightly kick, one leg up in the air while folding the other leg underneath. Either leg can be raised, it's up to the runner; neither one has a particular advantage as the lead leg. (If you have the player sit cross-legged, however, the leg that more naturally goes underneath first is the one that typically should also fold under when sliding.) Finally, when coming in to the base, the runner will hit the ground on either his rump, or perhaps one hip. The lead leg is the last part of the body to come down, and obviously it should do so on the base.

Sliding

Your better players should also learn how to execute arm hook slides. Such slides are particularly useful if the fielder already has possession of the ball, and the runner looks relatively certain to be tagged out. The procedure of sliding is the same—arms up, lean back, leg kick, one leg folds under, and hit the dirt. The difference here is that the runner should aim for a spot two to three feet away from, or behind, the base, and then attempt to hook his arm under the tag so that his hand, rather than his foot, makes contact with the base. Additionally, the runner may need to roll on his side in order to hit the brakes so that his hand isn't pulled off the bag. During practice, it's essential to drill your players on how to hold on during such a slide—an aggressive fielder will try to swipe the runner's hand off of the base, or sometimes the momentum from the slide itself makes it challenging to keep that grip. Arm hook slides are more difficult for fielders to handle, because the area to be tagged is more distant from their reach. There's less runner to tag.

Tagging Up

Beginning at around age eight, your players should become familiar with, and practice, tagging up on sacrifice flies. As described earlier, it's hard enough sometimes to convince some kids not to run on a fly ball with less than two outs. But for the more adept base runners, taking home from third on a sacrifice fly can be a sophisticated and relatively rare but exciting play. During the game, the third base coach should always remind the runner on third that a sacrifice fly could be an option on an outfield hit. Depending on the distance the batted ball travels—a short distance might be sufficient for an eight-year-old, but a longer distance, obviously, has to be achieved in a division of twelve-year-olds—the coach should teach his players to return to the edge of the bag, and then take off for home once that ball is secure in the outfielder's glove.

Specifically, instruct your runners to tag up on a deep fly ball to the outfield if they're on third base, or from either second or third on a deep fly ball particularly to right field.

Base running is an underrated aspect of baseball, yet it's potentially the easiest for young or less experienced players to master. As part of the overall concept of instilling your players, particularly your weaker players, with confidence, make base running an essential part of your practices. Let these weaker players, the ones who maybe don't bash the ball at the plate, lead the team in drills such as base relays, running the bases, sliding, running through first base, and running for extra base hits. These are vital skills for the entire team to learn but also offer perfect opportunities for the bottom of your order to feel as if they too have a chance to excel.

5

LEARNING HOW TO HIT THE BALL WELL

There are so many components to a good swing, which is what makes hitting well for a sustained period of time so difficult to maintain. As soon as a batter starts to focus on what's going wrong—turning his head, dropping his hands too low in the zone, lunging—the entire swing begins to suffer. Yet you have to isolate the problem in order to correct the hitch. So while hitting indeed is a series of many movements happening all at once, it's the fluid combination of all these acts that makes for a great hitter. That's why, as with everything else, batting practice is the most important thing.

Let's face it, for virtually all kids, hitting is the most exciting part of the game. Generally, they care where they are in the lineup a lot more than where they are in the field. But while some players crave the thrill that comes from cracking a nice hit and hearing the cheers from the crowd, others are petrified to step to the plate because they fear striking out yet again. Those are the players who need the most attention, and for them the basics must be taught from scratch.

A lot of children, surprisingly, swing bats that are too heavy for them. Choosing the right bat, in fact, may have a bigger impact on a child's game than any skill you can teach. Generally, of course, larger children should swing heavier bats than smaller children. But practically, until that player learns how to be an excellent hitter, everyone should be encouraged to use the lightest bat possible. Your players, at first, have to learn how to make contact and not hit for power. Since the heavier bats provide the potential for greater power, they shouldn't even be considered until the player has shown his ability to hit consistently.

Most youth baseball leagues require players to use only aluminum bats, and, even where you have a wood bat option, kids twelve or under should always choose aluminum because it will cause the hit ball to carry further. Wood bats are also usually too heavy for younger kids. Moreover, an aluminum bat won't cause the risk of a cracked bat and repeat trips to the sporting goods store for a replacement. And economic considerations are not insignificant—where you can typically purchase a very good bat for around $50-$75, some bats for kids can cost as much as $250.

For all players twelve and under, the diameter of the bat barrel ought to never exceed two and a quarter inches. As for length, of course, the longer the bat, the greater your reach to outside pitches. But length will also add weight, so your players need to choose carefully by swinging a variety of bats of different lengths. Generally, children age eight or below should use a bat that's twenty-six inches long, or less; kids around the age of ten can move up to a twenty-eight-inch bat; and by age twelve, depending on the size and strength of the player, a bat of approximately thirty inches in length ought to be about right.

The weight of the bat is really the most crucial consideration, especially for the younger ages. For some reason, though, bat manufacturers tend to use mysterious weight designations, such as –12. What does it mean if the bat you like is –12? Basically, that's the difference between its length (for example, thirty inches) and its weight (here, eighteen ounces). This would correspond to a relatively long but lightweight bat. Accordingly, a typical eight-year-old would do well with a sixteen to seventeen-ounce bat that registers somewhere around –9/–10 (twenty inches length). A ten-year-old should try swinging one that's heavier, perhaps eighteen to nineteen ounces or –10 (twenty-eight inches length), and a twelve-year-old, depending on his size (which, of course, can vary greatly), should be swinging a bat that weighs in at twenty to twenty-two ounces and therefore measures around –8 through –10 (thirty inches length). Unless the player weighs more than 150 lbs., a twenty-two-ounce bat should be sufficient.

One test to see if a bat is light enough is to have your player hold the bat by the handle with that arm extended straight out to his side. If the bat starts to shake or drop after less than fifteen seconds holding the bat in this way, then it's likely too heavy. Still, the very best way to determine the right bat weight for a child is to see how he or she performs with the respective bat length and weight. If they tend to swing too slow, the bat's probably too heavy. And if they swing too fast—that's good! You want your players to swing hard. Don't change a thing about that fast-swinging batter. Simply encourage them to increase their bat weight once you've helped them to establish consistent pitch contact, and it's time for them to gain more power.

Preparing to Hit

The majority of youth baseball hitters do not grip their bats correctly. Partly this is due to not having been taught how to grip the bat, and partly it's because the correct grip feels awkward at first, and so kids resist training themselves to do it the right way. Simply put, a batter

The proper grip

should grip the bat with their "door-knocker" knuckles lined up in a straight line.

These knuckles correspond to the second, or middle joints, of your fingers. Most kids gripping a bat will either line up the large knuckles of the hand or perhaps align the door-knockers of the top hand with the large knuckles of the bottom hand. The problem with this sort of incorrect grip is that the batter will tend to roll his hands while swinging and be inclined to hit down on the pitch—thus tending to produce ground balls. Swinging with your door-knockers lined up, however, will alleviate this tendency and ultimately allow the batter much better hand control during his swings.

Aligning the batter in the batter's box

A lot of young hitters don't know where to stand once they enter the batter's box and get ready to hit. Some stand too close to the pitcher, others too close to the plate. Many others, perhaps afraid of being hit, stand either too deep in the box or too far off the plate. A simple method to help position the batter correctly is to have him bend slightly while in the box and touch the outside of the plate with the end of the bat barrel.

If the batter can't reach the outside of the plate, then he's too far away; if it's too easy to reach, then he's too close. Coaches should help the batter to adjust his feet accordingly.

Next, make sure that the younger batter has his feet positioned toward the middle of the batter's box, with his front foot either

The stance

parallel to the front part of the plate or slightly behind it. The batter will learn to adjust his stance, according to his swing, as he gets older, but to start out most hitters should take their swings from the middle of the box. It's too difficult to hit fast pitching or relatively high pitches if they're too far out front, and it's extremely tough to hit either breaking pitches or low strikes if they're too far back. Hitting from the middle is a good place for younger hitters to start.

Although a batter's initial stance makes relatively little difference—what counts is how the batter is positioned as the pitch is delivered—it's advisable to teach your players to stand with knees somewhat bent and with a slight forward bend at the waist. Her feet should be square with her shoulders. The bat itself can either be right on the player's shoulder or a few inches above. Hands should be back but not tight on the bat. The key for this initial stance is that the batter should be as comfortable and as relaxed as possible, and the body balanced. The batter should be looking at the pitcher with eyes level, awaiting the windup and the pitch.

An open stance is where the batter places his front foot to the rear of his anchor foot, with his body somewhat open to the pitcher. A closed stance is where the batter's front foot is forward so that a right handed batter would be slightly more inclined to first base. While each of these have certain advantages for certain hitters (a dead pull hitter, for example, might compensate with a more open stance), start your less-experienced batters with a squared-up middle stance.

More important is that the batter, whichever his stance, has his eyes on the pitcher and, more specifically, on the ball. And make sure they are looking at that ball with both eyes! Some young hitters will squint with one eye or cock their heads to the side to focus on the eye that's closer to the pitcher. But such a view messes up the batter's depth perception and will encourage swings and misses. A batter needs both eyes on the ball, and on the same plane, to accurately see the pitch.

The load

Swinging the Bat

Once the batter is set, and the pitcher goes into his windup, the first move for the batter is to load. The load position, in which the batter's weight shifts back, the bat comes off the shoulder, and the hands are slightly raised, should be effected just before the pitcher releases the ball. At all times during the load, the batter's head does not move. If the load is initiated too late, then the batter will tend to swing late and miss.

What sorts of pitches should your batters swing at? Strikes. What sorts of pitches do younger baseball players often try to hit? Balls over their heads. Some kids can't lay off high pitches, and others flail at pitches in the dirt. When players get older and have more experience, a high strike can be a particularly tasty treat, because batters will learn how to drive those pitches. But at the younger levels, you need to keep reminding your batters to stay away from pitches they can't reach. They need to relax, stay focused and be patient at the plate.

If the batter decides to swing at a good pitch, then the next step in hitting is the stride. Striding, which follows the load, generally is an overrated element. It typically refers to a small step of no more than a few inches that a batter takes with his front foot, toward the pitcher, as the body weight shifts toward the front leg in preparation to hit. If your players do stride, then make sure it's a step of no more than six inches. Otherwise, they'll end up with their feet spread too wide and eliminate most of the power from below the hips. And if they're more comfortable not lifting that front foot—like Albert Pujols is—that's also perfectly fine.

More important for young hitters, during their swing, is that they don't lunge at the ball. It's obvious when this is occurring because the player will bend and lean his torso over the plate while swinging. This indicates a lack of confidence at the plate—what's really happening is that the batter is so afraid that he's going to miss the ball that he unconsciously is trying to get right on top of it as it comes in. Correcting a lunge is a very important part of a coach's job.

Instead of the torso entering the strike zone on a swing, it should be, at first, the hands leading the knob of the bat down to the ball. Some batters even attempt to almost blot out the image of the ball with the knob of the bat handle as the ball begins to approach the plate. Such an approach gets your hands, and ultimately the bat, in the right position—the front hand and elbow lead the bat into the zone while the back hand and elbow follow to power the swing. Right before the bat meets the ball, the arms should be fully extended, the weight shifted forward, the

The stride

The swing through the zone

hips turned by pivoting on the back foot, the front leg still and firm, the eyes focused directly on the ball, and, ideally, the ball should meet the barrel of the bat.

You'll know if the batter is turning his hips by the position of the back foot. That foot, while the hips are turning should be "squashing the bug." While the front foot is either striding or at least accepting the sudden shift forward in weight, it is still and locked in place during the swing; the rear foot, meanwhile, has turned on its toes in the direction of the pitcher.

The most crucial element in a young player's swing, however, is the position of his head. While the feet, hips, arms and body are moving, the head must remain still. You can easily tell when a batter has turned his head by observing his position at the end of the swing. If a right-handed batter hasn't turned his head, he'll end up after the swing looking over his right shoulder; if he's turned his head, he'll be looking

Squashing the bug

into space over his left. Conversely, a lefty batter should be looking over his left shoulder at the end of the swing, and not over his right.

If the batter turns his head, he is very unlikely to hit the ball because he won't be looking at it at the moment it should be meeting the bat. This, along with lunging, is the single biggest challenge that most youth baseball hitters have.

If you watch a youth baseball game, you will very likely hear from coaches to "keep your eye on the ball," or "watch the bat hit the ball," or some such similar refrain dozens of times during a game. The reason this is so is because it's difficult for kids to isolate the head from the rest of the body. It's not so simple to violently rotate everything except your head. It has to be taught by the coach and reinforced through batting practice.

Another element to watch for with young hitters is whether they're bailing out with the back foot, or "stepping in the bucket." Some inexperienced hitters, perhaps because they're afraid of getting hit, will fail to stride but rather step backwards, out of the box, with their back foot as they swing. There's virtually no way to successfully hit the ball like this because the batter's taking all the power and

Where the head should be	*Where the head should not be*

balance out of his swing. That batter is basically flailing at the ball with his arms. It takes some time to correct, because hitters that do this are generally doing it out of fear, but you have to train them over and over to keep that back foot staked to the ground.

At the moment that contact is made by bat on ball, the batter should be snapping and not turning over his wrists. This is the part of the swing where the batter will be happy that he lined up his hands along the door-knocking knuckles—you have almost no physical option but to snap if your hands are in this correct position, and it's almost impossible to otherwise turn them. Your bottom hand should be facing down as you hit the ball, and your top hand, or palm, facing up.

Also, at contact, the path of the bat ideally should be slightly upward so that the ball carries into either a line drive or deep fly ball. Some players hesitate at the moment of contact, but they instead need to learn to follow through. It's like running to first base—the destination isn't the base but somewhere past it. Similarly with batting, a player hasn't completed the swing when they've hit the ball. Rather, he has to follow through until the bat, generally, finds itself wrapped around his back. His head has turned to be looking over what was his rear shoulder at the start of the swing. Finally—don't forget to drop the bat and run!

Bunting

Most youth baseball coaches fail to teach players how to bunt, and in some of the younger divisions it's discouraged because leagues want those players to first learn how to swing the bat. But bunting is a very important skill to learn because, as your players get older, it gets harder and harder to score runs. The fifteen-fourteen games that you see with eight-year-olds generally become a thing of the past. Typically, a bunt is most useful when you're trying to push a runner across to the next base, or to steal home, but an occasional

The proper bunting technique

bunt is more often than not good for a hit when the opposing team is surprised.

To execute a bunt, the batter should turn in the box to face the pitcher in a very open stance. The top hand is placed about halfway down the bat with the thumb on top and the other fingers under-neath. Those fingers, to the extent possible, shouldn't be wrapped around but in a place where they can control the weight of the bat but not necessarily be hit when the pitch comes in. The bat is angled slightly up. As the pitch approaches, the batter should just make contact with it—don't push the bat, and don't pull it back, but almost try to simply catch it with the bat.

Hitting Drills

The best way for a player to practice is with a parent. This may not be of much comfort to the coach, who usually has at least twelve players to deal with at practice, but the truth is that it's hard to get everyone enough live batting practice because, if you're lucky, you've got no more than one backstop and one field.

Part of the coach's job is to get to know the parents of his players, and one of the main reasons to do this is so you can encourage them to get out there with their kids and practice.

Still, there are three very effective hitting drills you can work on with your team when you're all together on a practice field. Again, split the team into three stations. At the first station, have your players hit soft tosses into a fence. You do this by standing off to the side and tossing balls underhand to the player. This is a great time to fix the various hitting fundamentals, such as loading and footwork. It's also a perfect opportunity to gauge whether batters are lunging, or not using their hips effectively, or turning their wrists on the swing, or swinging with too much of an uppercut.

At a second station, work on hand-eye coordination by throwing a double soft toss. Here, you toss two balls simultaneously to the batter and call out which one of them you want them to hit. The batter has to act very fast, because the balls are already in the air. One will inevitably appear high, and the other lower. The drill forces batters to shorten their swings and trains them to stay back with a more compact swing, since the objective here is to make quick and solid contact.

If you're short of assistant coaches, you also can make this second station hitting off a tee. Here, your batter should take a normal stance but be positioned somewhat behind the tee. Especially use this drill to check that the batter's arms are extended and out in front of his body at the point of contact. As with the other hitting drills, have your players hit off of a tee and into a fence, if possible, to avoid having to chase down dozens of baseballs.

Finally, for the third station, pitch live batting practice to the rest of the team. Some coaches set up a batting machine, which certainly works, but that's not as effective as a living, breathing pitcher is for the batter's purpose of working on timing. Have a bucket of balls at your side, and mix your pitches—fastballs and changeups, varying speeds and locations. Have the players bunt on the first couple of pitches so they continue to hone that skill as well. There's no substitute for your batters than facing live pitchers. To the extent possible, pitch baseballs to them as much as you can.

The Mind of the Successful Hitter

As has been often said, hitting a baseball is one of the hardest things to do. Highly successful major league ballplayers succeed less than one-third of the time. The best youth baseball players may have a higher batting average than that, but they'll be all-stars if they even get on base half the time that they're up.

It's crucial for hitters, first, to not be afraid of the ball. In fact, their attitudes should be aggressive, at least in their minds. Encourage them to have a game plan when they face a certain pitcher—whether, for example, it's to take the first strike, or go in swinging away, or whether, for the older players, it's to wait on a fastball or a changeup. The pitcher is standing on the mound wanting to demolish your batter. Your batter has to dig in determined to crush the ball he's about to be thrown.

A successful hitter also has to stay calm, eliminate all mental distractions at the plate and focus slavishly on the ball. As Yogi Berra once asked, how can you think and hit at the same time? It takes discipline and a great deal of practice to be a good hitter, but it also takes patience and encouragement from the coach.

During the game, the coach needs to be vocal and cheer on his players, either from the bench or from a base coach box. Your worst hitters especially need such encouragement, not to mention extra attention. Don't only point out your players' mistakes, but be sure to encourage them about where they've improved—even if they end up with an out. If you have a player that strikes out often, congratulate him when he grounds out—that's improvement. Children in general need a lot of confidence, but children at bat need even more than usual. Help them to be better each time that they hit, and you'll make a huge stride toward building a winning team by season's end.

6

OFFENSIVE STRATEGIES

One of the most beautiful aspects of baseball is that you'll never see the same game twice. You can play 10,000 games, and each will be different; each will require a particular strategy. It's a complex sport, and strategies will change from game to game. So while training your players to run and hit is certainly the lion's share of your worth as an offensive coach, you also need to apply the best offensive strategies to help your team succeed. You certainly have to have quality at-bats and smart base running as the backbone of your offensive strategy. But a well-considered lineup also helps.

Although there's no precise science to structuring your batting order, even most casual observers of baseball know that you want speed and players with a high on-base percentage near the top of the lineup and your power hitters batting fourth through perhaps seventh. A lot of coaches might look at a fast kid on his team and conclude that he's a natural lead-off hitter. Or the strongest kid is the natural clean-up hitter. But, not only is that not always true, there are a few particular aspects unique to youth baseball worth considering.

At the youngest ages, especially, there tends to be a lot of strike-outs. To put it mildly, not all youth baseball players are good hitters. The kids that do get on base happen to be the ones who simply make contact. At age eight or below, because of relatively poor fielding and throwing, the batter who makes contact is at least as likely as not to reach base, even on an infield hit. For the most part, then, whether or not a batter can hit the ball—anywhere—should be your key criteria when arranging your lineup.

In youth baseball everyone has to bat, so you're certainly best served by placing your better hitters higher in the order. If you're lucky, and you drafted well, you'll at best have a fairly even split on your squad between kids who are inclined to hit a lot and those who strike out. You have to take this into consideration when crafting the lineup. Obviously, as the game progresses and the players bat through the order, you want your better hitters toward the top of the lineup so they can get the extra at-bats. The best hitter on your team should bat third. The next two best contact hitters, who ideally also have speed, should bat one-two. Traditionally, of course, your power hitter would bat fourth. This should be the case if your team is comprised of eleven- and twelve-year-olds but it's less of a factor at the younger ages because so few children are likely to hit a home run or even booming outfield hits. Rather, if you have another good contact hitter, have him bat fourth regardless of his power potential. After that, generally bat your players in order of how well they hit— unless your team is comprised of younger children.

Instead, for younger teams, once you've established your one-through-four hitters, try to alternate between other contact hitters and players who tend to strike out more often. The reason you'll benefit from this sort of a structure is because you want to keep your rallies going, and also extend the inning as long as possible. Putting up to bat two kids in a row who tend to strike out a lot is a good way to kill a rally. Putting up three strike out-prone kids could be a very fast inning—and you only have six of them. But if you sandwich these types of players around a batter who might not have as much strength but is better at putting the ball into play, then you have a good chance to score some runs. Again, below around the age of ten, most youth baseball players are still learning the fundamentals of the game. There are a lot of errors in the field. A kid who makes contact has a very good chance of reaching on an error. The kid who strikes out is just out.

At the older levels, or in more competitive leagues, where players are facing good pitchers, you may also want to consider varying your lineup between lefties and righties, if that's an option for you. The reason behind this is so the opposing coach doesn't try to take advantage by bringing in a left-handed reliever, for example, to face your three lefty batters in a row.

After your first couple of practices, it may be useful to privately rate the hitting abilities of your players on an A-through-D scale, with A being the best hitters and D reserved for the worst. When you draw up your first batting order, try not to have more than two A-rated players bat in a row, and try not to have any hitter follow any other hitter if he's more than two steps lower on your scale. In other words, if possible, an A should be followed by at least a B. It doesn't always work out that you can do this with your lineup, but this is a good rule of thumb to generally follow. It protects the better batters in your order, and it prevents you from bringing to bat three poor hitters in a row in any one inning.

In any case, your lineup generally should be fluid from game to game. Reward the players who get on base by moving them up in the order. Demote those who haven't been hitting the ball. Your players will recognize the logic and fairness of such a merit system, as long as you stick to it. In other words, don't subject everyone to this sort of a system except, for example, your own son. Holding your own kid to a different standard (by, say, batting him third every game even though he can't hit) is a surefire way to lose the support of your team. Kids know who's batting well and who isn't, and they typically won't complain at all if your lineup reflects what everyone can plainly see.

This isn't to say that every once in a while you shouldn't mix things up. If you've already clinched your playoff spot, for example, let some of the kids who typically batted near the bottom of the lineup a chance to hit up top. And if it's someone's birthday, sure, why not consider having the kid bat leadoff?

Youth baseball, especially in recreational leagues, is a place for kids to learn how to play the game and to have fun. Yes, you and they all want to win, but you need to balance that drive with a healthy sense of fairness, spontaneity and opportunities for your players to learn and be challenged.

A second smart offensive strategy that, for some reason, many coaches don't even bother to employ is the use of signs. Even at younger age levels, signs can be effective. Also, younger kids love learning the signs before a game, and the sharper ones will even remember to look for them while on base!

At the level of youth baseball, signs can be pretty simple—a touch to the nose, a fix of the cap, or a brush of the upper arm is generally enough. No one will be stealing your signs below age eleven, and, even if they do, it probably wouldn't matter. Once things get competitive at around age twelve, however, it's a good idea to either mask your signs with meaningless gestures or change them after every couple of innings.

One useful sign at younger ages is the take sign. There are a lot of walks when kids first start to pitch, usually at around age eight. With a three-zero count (or five-zero, depending on how many balls your league counts before issuing a walk at a respective age level), a lot of players either are bound and determined to swing away while they're in the box or perhaps don't realize that they can benefit from taking a pitch, even if it's a strike. And, to be honest, it's not especially cool for a coach to be shouting "take the next pitch" well within earshot of the opposing eight-year-old struggling on the mound. Some people involved with youth baseball might argue that kids should just be encouraged to swing whenever they get a strike. But taking a pitch in an attempt to work out a walk is an important skill that some players still have difficulty mastering as they get older.

In a related strategy, some coaches indoctrinate their players to always take the first strike, even if it's on the first pitch. Their justification is that this will allow their batters to get a sense of the pitcher, possibly put them ahead of the count, and also run up the pitch count. Still, your players are not the Boston Red Sox. If they give up the first strike, that's at least one-third of the good pitches they're going to see. For many hitters, that first strike will be the best pitch to hit. One more swing and a miss, and now your batter has to protect the strike zone. Not too many kids, though, are good enough to foul off close strikes. Accordingly, unless your players are very skilled, you're generally putting your offense at a significant disadvantage by teaching them to always take the first strike.

At the older levels, for sure, you'll want at least to give steal signs to your runners at first. Although players will have been trained to break for second after the catcher loses control of a pitched ball, there are other times when you, as coach, might want to test the opposing pitcher and catcher or simply try to move the runner to the next base without regard to whether the subsequent pitch will be wild. Your runner should be keyed in on the third base coach providing the signs and be confident enough to execute when he's given the green light. In more competitive leagues that allow leads, hit-and-run and bunt signs are also crucial for your players to learn.

Training your better players in the art of situational hitting is another offensive element that's often overlooked. It's really never too early to take some of your better batters aside and work with them on controlling their swings. For one thing, it's tough to manufacture runs in a division that doesn't allow leads and may not even allow steals. So, along with the bunt, having a few players attempt to hit, for example, behind a base runner can turn into a real offensive advantage for you. Most youth baseball coaches will have their runners on second hold on a grounder to the left side (provided, of course, that there's no one on first). But if you start to teach your better hitters in such situations to poke their hits behind the runner, that is to the right side of the infield, that runner on second can advance and be in better scoring position.

Your players should also, from an early age, learn how to take efficient leads on fly ball hits. Of course, their paramount concern has to be not getting picked off in a double play. But on a fly ball to left field, a runner on first should be able to advance halfway, or, depending on the dimensions of your playing field and the strength of the hit, even as much as three-quarters of the way to second base. Similarly, on a fly to either center or right fields, that same runner typically can advance at least a quarter of the way, and as much as halfway, to second base and still have time to get back safely.

Practicing when and how to get into a rundown, as described in detail as a drill in Chapter 12, is a further useful strategy that can help to create a run. Purposely relying on a rundown can allow lead base runners a chance to advance. And remember, if a base runner scores on two outs before another runner in a rundown is tagged out, that run will count. Rundowns, while of course risky, also increase the chances that an opposing team will make a bad throw or an error. In rare cases, too, a defensive player may get called for interference if he blocks your runner in a rundown.

At the older youth baseball levels, your players also should learn how to slide hard into second base to break up a double play.

Along with having a proper lineup, a set of signs and heads-up base running, a final helpful element to the offense is a spirited bench. Whether or not your players are on their feet and shouting encouragement to the batter and runners is, in part, a function of what sort of kids they are, the coach can certainly set the right tone. If you're quiet and kicked back on the bench, your players will tend to be as well. But if you're into it and expressive, and showing a lot of energy, that will inspire your players.

A spirited bench doesn't only help to nurture a winning attitude but it also subtly communicates that that's your attitude to the players on the opposing team. If your team means to win, it helps to show it. Moreover, if your players fight all the way, right to the last inning, even if they're down by several runs, you have kids that are winners no matter the final score of the game. A significant element of good youth baseball coaching is to teach your players how to never give up, how to fight to the last strike. The demonstration of that sort of spirit on the bench is something your players will carry with them for the rest of their lives.

7

THROWING AND PITCHING WITH GUTS

The defensive parts of baseball include, of course, pitching and fielding. But before a child can learn how to pitch, he first has to learn how to throw. Especially for younger children, throwing is neither easy nor comes naturally—it takes coordination of the entire body to throw a ball effectively. At first, many children throw off the wrong foot, so this is the first and most obvious throwing error a coach should correct.

Throwing off the wrong foot

The foot that corresponds to the glove hand is the one that should step during the throwing motion. Have your very inexperienced players first practice by throwing off the correct foot. Ideally, the player should learn to take two small steps, or crow hops—the glove foot, the anchor foot, and then, as the weight shifts forward, a longer stride with the glove foot again—before releasing the throw. Additionally, that glove foot should be pointed in the direction of the targeted fielder.

Meanwhile, the elbow of the throwing hand needs to be raised up, bent, and well behind the shoulder. The ball should be gripped by its seams and the player's fingers on top of the ball. The forearm of the throwing hand then stretches back as the glove hand points forward, and the wrist also should be loose and back. Just prior to the release,

The correct throwing motion

the player should thrust the throwing arm in a forward sweep, over the shoulder, while whipping both the elbow into a locked position and finally the wrist forward. Just like running to first or swinging the bat, follow through after the release is crucial to a good throw in order to generate velocity. Finally, that back leg will swing forward along with the full weight of the player's body. The throwing shoulder should end up facing the player intended to field the ball.

Ideally, the player learning to throw a ball ought to grip it lightly and with his fingertips on the seams; it's harder to throw well if you hold the ball deep in the palm of your hand. The whipping action of the wrist is important to throw a ball well, and coaches of younger children ought to pay close attention to whether their players struggling to throw are trying to do so with a stiff wrist. If so, correct it—the snap of the wrist at the end of the throwing motion is vital both for accuracy and acceleration.

A good drill for young throwers is to have them pair off in two lines facing each other, perhaps ten feet apart. Each player should take a knee and work on tossing the ball back and forth. The knee-down position takes the legs out of the throw and allows the player to isolate the arm motion. In turn, the exercise allows the coach to observe whether the arm angle is correct and whether the player is both holding the ball correctly and whipping his wrist efficiently.

Effective Pitching

Those of your players who do throw well should be encouraged to pitch. Pitching, however, is not merely a matter of technique. A big, big part of the pitching game is in the head. Excellent pitching, in fact, depends somewhat less on what goes on with the player's arm but more with what's between the ears.

No one, not even guys like Tim Lincecum or Roy Halladay, pitches well every time out. The difference between throwing a ball well and becoming a pitcher, therefore, has a lot to do with a player's emotional state. When good young pitchers become rattled, they begin to pitch poorly. When they get emotional on the mound or start to cry, they fail to throw strikes. Some kids are so good at pitching but when they walk one or two players they tend to fall apart, and, before you know it, five runs have come in. The question you need to ask is what is the mindset of your best pitcher? How does he handle on the mound the ups and downs of a game, the bad calls, the errors by his fielders?

Your pitcher necessarily has to be a good teammate, not getting down on his fielders when they make an error and not arguing with the umpires. This isn't only a matter of decent sportsmanship, but it's vital in order to get an effective game out of your pitcher. Anyone who lets this sort of bad stuff get into their heads will not have the consistency to win. Coach your pitcher to pick up his teammates after a bad play. Teach them to not show any frustration. And train them to forget about the last play—if it was bad, then flush it down the figurative toilet. It's the next batter now that matters.

If the pitcher is upset with the umpire's strike zone, then either you or your catcher has to find out what that umpire considers a strike, and then your pitcher has to throw it there. If the pitcher's upset that the catcher lets a few balls get away, then tell him to stop throwing them in the dirt. An effective pitcher must, in effect, be stoic, communicating nothing discouraging to his teammates and nothing useful to the other side. More than anything, the pitcher's attitude must stay aggressive: The batter that's coming up will be defeated; he will not get on base; he will not even touch my stuff. Your pitchers have to be tough.

Pitching, therefore, is mentally exhausting. But it's also more physically fatiguing than any other position except, perhaps, catcher. In other words, the pitcher's body also has to be sufficiently prepared. Both long-tossing and stretches are vital to protecting your pitchers' good arms.

Whether before practice or a game, your pitchers should start by stretching. Any number of stretching programs could be effective but the following, which you should perform together with your pitchers, are particularly recommended:

- Stretch the calves by leaning against a fence with one foot forward. The rear foot should be flat on the ground, and the stretch should be felt in that rear calf. Repeat for the other leg.
- Stretch the hamstrings by lying on your back, bending one knee, and then pulling that knee toward your head. Repeat for the other leg.
- While still on your back, bend both knees with your feet flat on the ground. Keeping your knees together, lean your legs down to one side and hold; then switch to the other side.
- Lie down flat on your back and hold your arms straight out on the ground, as if you were about to make a snow angel. Roll one slightly bent leg over the other, and twist your head and upper body in the opposite direction. Then switch to the other side. This is a great stretch for your lower back and obliques.
- To stretch your throwing shoulder, stand, fold your locked throwing arm across your chest, place your other hand above the elbow of that throwing arm and pull until you feel the stretch in the small muscles around the shoulder joint.
- Following these stretches, have your pitchers run. They should start slowly and work their way up to faster laps. After no more than ten minutes of running they should begin their throwing program.

Start by pairing off your pitchers and have them throw lightly to each other at no more than twenty feet apart. They should not move their legs at all—no striding, no stepping, and certainly no windups. After a few minutes of this, have them back up about ten feet. Continue these drills, without using their legs, retreating another ten feet every few minutes until they're about fifty feet apart. At that distance, your pitchers should bring in their legs and start to stride. Over the next ten minutes, continue to have them increase the distance of their throws. A long toss will of course differ between players of different ages, but if your team is around eleven or twelve years old, your kids should be tossing, for the purpose of these drills, at a maximum of between seventy-five to one hundred feet.

Once this program is completed, your pitchers are warmed up and ready to add their mechanics—including the windup.

The Pitching Windup

Feet against the front of the rubber

Most youth baseball players should learn two varieties of windup—the full delivery and the stretch. Although younger pitchers prefer generally to pitch out of a stretch, which is normally employed when there are runners on base, a baseball coach with foresight will start teaching the full windup right from the beginning.

There are six key steps to the windup. Before any movement, however, the pitcher should be set up standing square to the catcher, with his feet on the edge of the rubber.

The ball should be in his throwing hand, and both that hand and the ball are tucked inside of his glove. The glove may be raised close to the pitcher's chest, or as high as his face to the point where the pitcher is just staring over the top of the webbing. While in the glove, the pitcher's fingers should be placed precisely on the ball in preparation for the pitch he's about to throw (generally, for youth baseball purposes, either a fastball or a changeup). This is the ready position.

The first part of the windup is the step back. Here, the foot that corresponds to the glove hand takes a small step either back or to the side, at an approximately seventy-five degree angle. The weight should simultaneously transfer to this stepping leg. It's important,

The pitcher's ready position

Windup/step back

however, for coaches to make sure that this first step back isn't too long and definitely not too far back. If it is, then the pitcher will likely become unbalanced later in the windup, causing him to lean on one side or the other in order to compensate. This first stage is a small step for the purpose of shifting a pitcher's weight in preparation for the upcoming pivot.

Step two is to pivot on the other foot, the one that corresponds to the throwing hand. Here, the foot simply turns to be parallel to the rubber; it's a small pivot, at most ninety degrees, on the heel. At this point the pitcher's weight will start to shift from the back foot to the front in preparation for the kick.

Step three of the windup is the kick. Once the body weight has shifted back to this anchor leg, the rear (or side) leg should start to lift, marking the beginning of the kick. At this point most pitchers will also lift their arms to some point above their chest; this is the

Windup/pivot

Windup/the kick

stage where many major league pitchers, of course, lift their hands as far as over their heads. For maximum balance, the kick should be relatively high—that thigh should be at least roughly parallel to the ground. Also, at this stage, the pitcher's body is now fully sideways to the plate. The leg on the rubber shouldn't be locked but slightly bent at the knee. There's no need for the pitcher to freeze in this position at anytime. Rather, the windup, although consisting of distinct steps, should be fluid and always in motion. It's even okay if the pitcher at this stage is leaning in a bit toward the batter.

Step four is the stride forward. Here, the throwing hand begins to separate from the glove as the kicking leg starts to stride toward the plate. When the throwing arm drops back, however, the pitcher's body shouldn't necessarily fall immediately toward the plate—that will cause the delivery to be late and the stride out of rhythm. Rather, the pitcher actually rocks back slightly toward second base, keeping the balance on that anchoring leg and causing the front hip

Windup/the stride

to momentarily rise higher than the rear hip. But be careful: this shouldn't be an exaggerated lean back toward second base—instead, it's a subtle move to hold the torso ever so slightly in check as the front leg, alone, strides toward the plate.

At this point, the anchoring leg starts to push. Power pitching comes not from the arm, but from the lower body, and so strong legs are crucial for pitchers. As the front leg strides, the back leg pushes off the rubber. This motion causes the hips to swivel, a further source of power that results in greater velocity for the throw. The pitcher here doesn't need to suddenly bend that back knee, as some kids do, with the idea that this move will generate more power. It won't generate power; instead it will throw the windup out of rhythm and ultimately affect the accuracy of the throw in an unintended way. At the end of the stride, the front foot should land at a comfortable distance, far enough away from the body to stabilize the pitcher's balance but not so far that he ends up coming down on his heel or falling to the side. At the same time, the stride shouldn't be too short, because a short stride will diminish the power he can maximize from his legs and hips. Ideally, the front toes should be pointed straight at the catcher and the foot itself ought to end up somewhere off-center in the direction of the pitcher's glove-hand side.

The fifth step is to release the pitch. As the stride is completed and all the body weight pours forward into the front leg, the arm follows either over the shoulder or at a three-quarters position. As the pitch is released, all of the body's weight and force drives into the throw,

Windup/the push-off

Windup/the release

Windup/the finish

and the back leg comes around and lands somewhat parallel to the front foot.

The completion of the windup is itself the sixth step. The pitcher needs to finish out front, balanced, and ready to field.

The Stretch

A pitcher will work from the stretch position when a runner is on base, to shorten the time, as compared to the windup, that the runner might otherwise have to run. Of course, a lot of younger players (and even some older ones, including major leaguers) prefer to pitch at all times from the stretch, and that's perfectly fine. There's no need for

Stretch/foot on the rubber

the coach to insist on pitching from the windup as long as they're pitching effectively.

As a modified windup, the stretch has some of the same steps that a windup has. The pitcher starts with his rear foot at the edge of and parallel to the pitching rubber, with his weight on that back leg.

The throwing hand, which is precisely gripping the ball in preparation for a specific type of pitch, should be tucked in the glove as the arms are relaxed near the waist.

From this ready position, go straight into the leg kick. It should be a relatively high kick, as with the windup, and the back knee is slightly bent. For pitchers that throw both out of the windup and the

Stretch/ready position

Stretch/leg kick

stretch, the leg kick should be in the same position and same height for either method of delivery.

After this point in the motion, every step follows as it would for the windup: Stride forward, drop the throwing arm back, thrust with the back leg, open the hips, bring the throwing arm forward, release the pitch, follow through, and prepare to field.

Gripping the Pitches

Although pitchers and their pitching coaches have developed a multitude of different sorts of pitches, recreational youth baseball players should only deliver three: the four-seam fastball, the two-seam fastball, and the changeup. The first pitch to teach, and the only one that you should encourage young pitchers to stick to until they throw it accurately, is the four-seamer. This is the primary pitch for youth baseball.

To grip the four-seam fastball, have your pitchers place their index and middle fingertips across the seams of a baseball so that a half-circle or horseshoe-shaped seam faces into the ring finger of the throwing hand. The thumb then goes beneath the baseball. The index and middle fingers, which now cross the seams in four places, are ideally approximately a half-inch apart. If they're too far apart your pitcher will sacrifice velocity. To experiment with adding a bit of a break to the pitch, your pitcher can place these two fingers slightly off-center.

The ball should be held lightly. A lot of young pitchers, when they get nervous or tense, start to squeeze their pitches. Their arms get tight, and the result of all this tension is a lot of pitches in the dirt. The four-seam fastball should be held in a very relaxed grip, almost as if your pitcher is going to throw an egg, with a gap between the ball and the palm of the hand. This isn't especially easy for younger children to execute because their hands are small; nevertheless, as they get older, it's a very important component of the pitch. The pitcher, when he releases the throw, should have the ball somewhat roll off his fingertips at the seams. As the ball approaches the batter,

The four seam grip

The two seam grip

a well-thrown four-seamer creates the impression that it's rising in the zone.

A two-seam fastball is the second important grip for a young pitcher to learn. It's similar to the four-seam fastball but, when thrown correctly, sinks as it approaches the batter. The index and middle fingers are placed on top of the most narrow seams of the baseball. The thumb is secure on the bottom of the ball in between the seams.

Unlike the four-seamer, the two-seam fastball should be gripped tightly. The tighter grip, in part, is what gives this pitch its sink. It's a great pitch for a right hander to throw inside to righties because it tends to tail in toward the pitcher's throwing hand side. Similarly, left handers find it very effective against lefty batters.

The third pitch coaches should teach to their best pitchers is a three-finger changeup. The changeup is also known as an off-speed pitch. When thrown correctly, the changeup appears to the batter to be coming off of the pitcher's hand as a fastball. The pitch, however, is considerably slower. Accordingly, the batter's timing likely will be off when he starts to swing. When a smart pitcher sets up his changeup by first pitching a good fastball, the batter often will be fooled into swinging early.

To grip a three-finger changeup, have your pitcher place his middle three fingers across the seams at the top of the ball with their thumb and pinky on the smooth part of the ball underneath. It's up to the pitcher whether to allow those bottom fingers to touch each other—it's a question of comfort, and whether or not those fingers touch is fine either way.

The changeup, unlike either fastball, should be gripped deep in the palm, which is one of the keys to slowing the velocity of the delivered pitch. Additionally, the pitcher's wrist should be stiff and with much less of the snap or whipping action that is needed for a fastball delivery. The essence of throwing the changeup is that it's delivered exactly as if it were a fastball—encourage your pitchers to throw it hard, with the same arm angle, at the same arm speed, and with even the same looks on their faces as they release it.

These three pitches should serve your pitchers very well through the age of twelve. For those most advanced pitchers, consider teaching them circle changeups and sliders as well, but never a curveball. Some recently published studies claim that throwing a curveball doesn't necessarily damage the arms of youth baseball pitchers, but why take a chance? If your pitcher can throw consistent strikes with

The changeup grip

two fastballs and a changeup, he will be among the very best pitchers in your league.

Covering First Base and Home

Important fielding strategies to teach your pitchers are covering first base on a groundball to the right side and covering home if a pitch gets away from the catcher with a man on third.

If a grounder is hit to the first baseman that pulls him relatively far off the bag, then the pitcher has to be ready to dart off of the mound to take the throw at first. When the batter first makes contact, the pitcher should begin his move. The path to first base isn't especially straight; rather, it's an approach like an arc, or a banana, as he curves his way over to the bag, veering closer to the first base line at the start of his approach. The advance to first base from this path will help the pitcher to avoid a collision with the base runner. As the pitcher reaches first and prepares to take the throw, his foot should always aim for the inside, front corner of the base. If he steps directly on the base, or on the far side, he very likely will obstruct and collide with the runner. After fielding the ball and making sure that his foot is simultaneously on the bag, the pitcher should keep running past the base to both slow his momentum and to get out of the way. The pitcher will very likely need to turn, sometimes awkwardly, to avoid the base runner, so this is a play that coaches should drill a lot in practice.

Especially in recreational youth baseball leagues, where pitches often escape the gloves of catchers, pitchers must be very alert to cover home with a man on third. In divisions where stealing home is allowed, a runner on third will eagerly anticipate a ball in the dirt getting away from the catcher. That catcher, now in a panic, will often stray far from home to recover the live ball, giving the third base runner time to rush home. If the pitcher doesn't cover home, that runner will likely be safe. Just the sight of the pitcher breaking for home, however, will cause the third base runner to pause and possibly prevent the steal.

Pickoffs

In many youth baseball leagues, even up through the age of twelve, leads are not allowed, and pickoff attempts won't be made. However, if your league does allow leading and pickoffs, then you must train your pitchers how to hold the runners on base. There are a lot of ways to do this—throwing over to keep the runner close, holding onto the ball longer than usual in the stretch, stepping off the rubber, or the occasional pitchout to the catcher.

In a good pickoff move, the pitcher will rotate his throwing shoulder, break his hands just before he starts the kick and throw with a short arm movement. A right handed pitcher has to develop somewhat of a slide-step in order to fool the runner at first base. However, left-handed pitchers have an advantage because they can go either to first or pitch to the batter out of their usual leg kick without the tipoff of a slide-step.

Whether righty or lefty, the pitcher with a runner on first should be gazing, when at the set position, halfway between first and home. It's important to do this every time so the runner can't judge a pitcher's intention based on the movement of his head. In any event, with runners on base, the pitcher should never have predictable moves. He needs to mix up his strategies to always keep the runners guessing and tentative.

Your pitchers, and your catcher, are in so many ways extremely important members of your team. Depending on the availability of your players, and the opportunity to have access to field space, coaches should consider having weekly pitchers-and-catchers practices in addition to at least one full-team practice every week.

8

TEACHING CHILDREN TO CATCH AND FIELD

For young children, catching even a slow-moving ball on the ground is not as easy as it seems it should be. The five- and six-year-old kids playing T-ball, for sure, are all eager to chase the ball and catch it, and many even run in from the outfield to make a play at the pitcher's mound. But whether or not it's an instinctive reaction to protect themselves from harm, most don't know how to naturally field a ground ball. They tend to try to squash it with their mitts. Like a cat stopping a mouse, most small children will come down with their paws on top of the ball, trying to trap it underneath the glove as if it might dart out once they peek underneath. So catching has to be taught.

Fielding Groundballs

Fielding grounders is a good place to start teaching a child who's new to baseball, because most kids have loved to chase after a rolling ball since they were toddlers. If your players are very young and completely new to the game, have them get down on one knee to start fielding softly tossed balls on the ground. The first skill they should learn in this regard is "alligator hands." As the ball approaches, the glove hand should be down to the ground, and the free hand over it, forming something similar to an alligator's mouth—the base of the hands serve as a fulcrum trapping the ball as it ideally rolls into the glove.

As mentioned above, what you want to break here is the habit many children have of coming down with the glove to squash the ball from above. Rather, the baseball should easily glide right into the mitt and be prevented from either rolling up the player's arm or otherwise escaping by the free hand. Of course, the player eventually needs to learn how to keep the glove down and center her body on

Alligator hands

the oncoming grounder, but start the youngest players with gently rolling balls aimed right at the glove.

Once the ball is tucked into the mitt, the kid has to do something with it. In other words, she has to know to throw it, typically to first base. Therefore, once the player fields the ball, she should pull it either to her belt or to her chest in preparation to throw.

This should be considered step two in learning how to field a grounder. A lot of younger or less-experienced children will know

Pull to belt/chest

they have to throw the ball but will have no idea how to successfully execute the move. What you end up seeing therefore, mostly in the T-ball or 7s divisions, are wild throws to nowhere in particular, often off the wrong foot, and sometimes traveling no more than a few feet.

Pulling the fielded ball to the belt area allows the players to set themselves up for the throw. The next step is the actual execution of the throw. From the belt (or chest), the fielder will point his glove hand in the direction of the fielder who is to receive the throw, and draw back his throwing hand, which is holding the ball in a T position. The pointed glove provides the body with balance and also helps the child to toss the ball in the correct direction. The T position sets up the correct over-the-shoulder throw.

The throw

The T position

Youth baseball players, sometimes even as old as eleven or twelve, need to be reminded to throw over the shoulder and not side-armed.

For some reason, a lot of kids must think it looks cool to make sidearm throws from the infield—after all, that's how a lot of MLB players do it. But because most children have difficulty controlling their aim, not to mention the trajectory and velocity of a throw, it's much more effective to encourage them at the earliest ages to do it the correct way. When kids throw sidearm, they end up bending awkwardly and losing their center or balance, which results in a weak and usually inaccurate throw. Over the shoulder throws allow for greater control and accuracy.

The proper throw and release

The incorrect sidearm throw and release

So your young fielder has fielded the grounder with alligator hands, pulled the ball to their midsection, and prepared for the throw by bringing their arms into the T position. Now, he brings his arm over the shoulder and releases in the direction of the receiving fielder.

One of the keys to fielding groundballs, particularly at the early learning stage, is to continually remind your players to keep their gloves down. So many hard-hit balls get through to the outfield because the player, either due to laziness or because he expected the ball to have a bigger hop, did not get low enough to put the glove on or close to the ground, and it skittered underneath.

Another key is to train your players to center their bodies on the incoming groundball. First, it's easier to field a ball that approaches the center of your body, rather than one that goes either to your left or right or demands a backhanded play. Second, the player's body itself acts to block a grounder that might otherwise get away. If they can't catch it outright, then every fielder in baseball wants to keep that ball in front them as the next best option. It gives them the chance to recover quickly and still throw the runner out. Once that ball gets behind the fielder, though, the chance of making a smooth play is virtually eliminated.

The ready position

An effective drill for the young fielder is to teach him to field grounders from very short distances. Have him field with alligator hands, and then pull the ball to his belt/chest area and look up. You have to train them to look in the direction into which they're throwing, otherwise the ball will arbitrarily sail off into the wind.

Agility also has to be encouraged when fielding grounders. Teach them the ready position.

Here, the player ideally is on his or her toes, with knees slightly bent, hands at the side and generally relaxed but alert in anticipation of a play. Being on his toes with slightly bent knees allows the fielder to easily break to the left or right, as well as forward or backward. In fact, every defensive player, and not just the infielders, should be on their toes and never on their heels.

A fun drill for younger players is to split the squad into two lines and have each pair of players face each other. One player rolls a grounder to his or her opposite partner, and the fielder then goes through the process of pulling it to their belts, raising their arms to a T position and firing the ball back the other way. After each throw, the players reverse the process. For older kids, the players can shuffle down the field after each throw, pairing with different players and keeping the momentum of the drill fast.

Catching Balls in the Air

Many of the same young children who happily chase grounders are a lot more afraid of baseballs flying toward them in the air.

Most players, when they begin to learn how to catch, instinctively try to catch all throws with a basket catch. As such, they turn their glove hand with palm toward the sky and expect the ball to plop right in. Children prefer to catch this way at first because if the ball does find its way into the glove, it's not likely to slip out. Catching a throw straight-on, however, requires the player to squeeze the mitt once the ball enters the pocket. At first, most of these throws will be dropped. So the child, who does not want to repeatedly fail, will hesitate to catch the ball correctly until he or she becomes more confident about proper catching technique. The other reason children won't catch a ball straight on is that they're afraid of missing it and getting hit.

Catching a ball, like so many baseball skills, is perhaps half psychology, half technique. Start to teach your players how to catch by first making them comfortable. Begin by tossing underhand to them at very short distances. Once they feel confident that the ball won't necessarily hurt them, begin to explain how to position their glove hands. A basket catch is appropriate when the incoming ball will reach them below the belt.

Basket catch

A standard catch, in which the arm is outstretched, the wrist bent, and the mitt open to the oncoming ball is best when the throw comes in above the belt. This actually takes a lot of practice before it becomes natural to the young player. The reason is, again, because many young players are afraid to be hit by the ball. As with all catches, the beginning fielder should be instructed to always use two hands.

Once your players become comfortable fielding grounders and fly balls, also drill them in making backhanded catches. The same kids who finally stopped trying to catch everything straight to their

Standard catch

chests with a basket catch will suddenly turn their wrists and make a stab at balls in the air approaching their throwing sides in a sort of awkward, reverse basket-catch manner. Make sure the palm in their glove hands is not pointed up toward the sky; rather, that palm should be held either to the side or straight up to field a ball in the air on a backhanded play.

Some children, perhaps with good reason at first, are afraid of the ball. They may have been hit with a ball in the past or they may lack confidence in their ability to catch it. Of course, this fear eventually recedes after enough practice. But to start to alleviate their concerns, begin by taking a very soft ball and throw it into their chest. A sponge ball, of course, is too soft for this purpose, but a tee-ball division ball is soft enough to not hurt but baseball-looking enough to still make the worried child just a little bit apprehensive.

During practice, especially for younger children, be certain to pair off your players appropriately. Some eight-year-olds, for example, throw hard; other eight-year-olds can barely catch. Put the hard throwers with kids of similar abilities, who can catch those sorts of throws. And group the players with less ability together so that they aren't so vulnerable to hard-thrown balls.

Pop-ups and fly balls pose challenges as well. Again, the new player has to overcome his or her fear of being hit on the head. How should you help them to overcome this fear? By hitting them on the head with a ball.

Whether fielding in the infield or the outfield, your defensive players need to learn how to catch fly balls by lining them up as if they were trying to have the ball strike them in the head. As mentioned earlier, a great drill to help make your players familiar with the technique is to toss a wiffle ball high in the air and instruct your players not to catch it—but to bounce it off of their heads. They learn, first, not to fear the ball. Second, they become familiar with how to line up a fly ball to be caught. Follow the wiffle ball drill with fly ball drills using a real baseball. Instruct the players to line up the ball as if it was to hit them in the head, but to this time get their gloves out in front, around a foot above and in front of their faces, to catch the ball. These are essential repetitive drills that are necessary to teach kids how to correctly catch.

One of the more difficult techniques for children to learn is how to go back on a ball when it appears to be trending behind them. Most players will backpedal, lose their balance, and either trip or just fail to catch the ball. Whether an infielder or an outfielder, the proper way to go back on a fly ball is to turn sideways, keeping an eye on the ball, and retreat in a sidestep motion. It's not an easy play, but when you get under the ball, then line it up and extend your glove hand for the catch.

If the ball is obviously way over your head, the player should more aggressively turn, run, and then look up to find it.

An effective drill to develop this technique somewhat resembles a quarterback-receiver football play. Have your player run with his

Going back on a fly

back to you at least for twenty yards, then turn toward you and look up to find the high fly ball, which already had been tossed while they were running. The drill teaches the players to be alert and to be quick in locating fly balls.

Instructions for Outfielders

Outfielders, like infielders, also have a "ready" position. Ideally, when the pitcher prepares to deliver a pitch, outfielders should be positioned on their toes, with the leg corresponding to the glove hand slightly in front and knees relaxed and perhaps a bit bent. This ready position gives the player the maximum ability to quickly move in any direction upon a hit—to the left, right, forward or back. As with all defensive players, it's especially crucial to be on your toes—that's the position that allows you to best respond. No one fields well when they're flat-footed!

Outfielder ready position

As with infielders going back on pop-ups, it's preferable for outfielders to run back sideways, with a side-step, to retreat on a fly ball. But there's a lot of room to cover for an outfielder, so at times, when a ball is hit deep and way over the outfielder's head, it's best to turn and run, estimating the trajectory of the ball and then seeking to find it quickly by turning back to look up.

Outfielders also have particular approaches to fielding a ball on the ground. Where possible, and if moving slowly enough, the ball should be picked up by the outfielder with his bare hand and then thrown quickly back to the cut-off man. Getting rid of the ball fast is especially crucial at younger ages. For some reason, younger outfielders tend to hold on to the ball—perhaps insecure about where to throw it—as the runners merrily circle the bases. Teach your outfielders to get the ball back to the infield, and preferably to the cut-off man, as quickly as possible.

When fielding a harder-hit ball on the outfield grass, the outfielder should be prepared to snag it with his glove, and, in a fluid motion consisting of no more than a couple of steps, retrieve the ball with his throwing hand and throw it back in using the momentum gained by charging the ball to get some acceleration on the throw.

Outfielder charging ball on ground

The first step that an outfielder takes when preparing to run down the ball is vital. Once the ball is hit, and he determines the direction he must run, the outfielder has to not only step in that direction with his lead foot, establishing the angle he needs to run, but also pivot on the anchor foot in the direction toward which the ball is heading. If that anchor foot remains pointed toward the batter, the outfielder will break awkwardly and lose precious time toward creating the most efficient route.

An easy drill for your players to work on this drop step and develop efficient outfield running routes is to line up your outfielders at the edge of the outfield grass. One by one, the coach will shout to each player the direction he wants that player to run (left, right, straight back, etc.). The player will then turn, making sure the pivot foot rotates as well, and begin to run the route. The coach will follow by either throwing or hitting a high fly ball, allowing the fielder sufficient time to read the play and get under it. That player then returns the ball to the coach's bucket and takes a place at the end of the line.

Also coach your outfielders with respect to how to catch a fly ball when there are runners on base. In these sorts of situations, and if he has time, the outfielder ideally should line himself up a few feet behind where the ball is to be caught, and then step up on the ball as it descends, thus gaining the acceleration needed to throw the ball strongly and immediately back into the infield. This approach, in which the outfielder takes no more than a step and throws, saves some precious time that would otherwise be wasted taking some extra steps for momentum, particularly when a base runner has tagged up in an attempt to advance.

Reinforce for your outfielders the lesson that under most circumstances they should never backpedal. If the ball's trajectory will require more than a couple of steps back, that fielder should always turn and side-step until he's under it.

Instructions for First Basemen

First base is a vital, yet underrated, position. For some reason, it's usually the position where coaches tuck their overweight kids or their left-handed players. It's true to some extent that the corner infield positions require a bit less physical exertion than other positions, but chubby first basemen have no inherent advantage. On the other hand, a left-handed first baseman is somewhat preferable to a right-handed one, although there are plenty of great righty first basemen, including such recent repeat Gold Glove fielders as Albert Pujols and Mark Teixeira.

When your players are young (eight or under), you have to be sure that whomever you put at first base can capably catch a hard-thrown ball. As we've observed, there are always a few kids who can throw harder than most of the rest of the team. More to the point, there are always a few kids who can throw harder than most of the rest of the team can catch. Serious injury can result if you have a kid at first base who isn't at least capable of protecting his or her face. So it's not the one position into which you would rotate any player. Unlike, for example, second base, it's not the ideal position to introduce your least capable fielders to the infield.

First base is always an important position, but it becomes increasingly challenging for older players, especially once your local league rules allow for leads and base-stealing. When holding a base runner on, the first baseman—whether left-handed or a righty—should be positioned in a way so that his right foot either touches, or is very close to, the inside portion of first base.

The first baseman's glove is outstretched, giving the pitcher a good target. If the pitcher fires the ball over in a pickoff attempt, the first baseman catches the throw and applies the tag to the returning runner with a sweeping motion.

This is one of the advantages of being a left-handed first baseman—the glove is on the right hand and thus a bit closer to the runner. Lefties, however, do feel somewhat awkward at first having their right feet as the anchor beside the bag. They especially need to practice receiving pickoff throws because they will tend to want to anchor the bag with their left feet. However, this latter position is much less desirable than a right foot anchor, because it will result in the first baseman having to turn his body to position himself for the tag. At first base, especially, footwork is everything.

Tagging the runner

The Catcher

The catcher's responsibilities are almost nonexistent at age eight or below, where few players can even catch a pitch, and where the biggest thrill for the player is simply in wearing all the armor—the chest protector, the shin guards, the cup, and the mask. The catcher, however, becomes incredibly important once base stealing is allowed and kids are pitching all six innings of a ballgame. In fact, beginning by around age nine, the catcher becomes the quarterback of the team.

At the younger ages, it's recommended to let everyone on the team have a chance to catch. Of course, for boys, it's essential that they're wearing a cup before you put them back there, but it's a position with lots of action and, at least at the youngest ages, otherwise no chance of getting hurt. All that equipment protects them, even if the ball hits them in the face, and the position gives a young child the chance to practice fielding relatively hard incoming throws (or pitching machine tosses).

The catcher is positioned on his toes, in a crouch, although to be most efficient that crouch should not be too deep but rather slightly raised so that he's ready to spring up in case of a foul pop up or base stealer. Depending on where the catcher (or the coach) wants the ball to be thrown, the catcher gives the pitcher a clear target with his wide-open, oversized glove. His body should always be square to the pitcher.

The catcher, ideally, should also be positioned as close to home plate as possible without risking the chance of his mitt or, worse, his head being hit by a swinging bat. (A hit mitt will cause a catcher's interference call, and the batter will be awarded first base.) A lot of children position themselves, of course, as far away as possible from the batter, but this poses a huge disadvantage for your pitcher because he has to throw the ball further. A catcher positioned close to the plate also helps the umpire to more accurately call strikes.

When there's no runner on base, the catcher's throwing hand should be relatively out of the way so it's not easily injured by a foul tip. Different catchers have different methods, but that free hand can be either tucked behind the buttock or the back. When a runner is on base, however, that throwing hand needs to come a bit more forward in preparation to throw out the runner. With a runner on base, the throwing hand moves closer to the action and is best tucked under the catcher's thigh.

When throwing out a runner on a caught pitch, as opposed to one that got away, the catcher springs up from his crouch and immediately assumes a throwing position, with his left foot forward (for righties) and his anchor foot in the rear.

Without taking a step, and without tearing off the mask, the efficient catcher cocks his arm back with the ball in his throwing hand approximately near his ear. That position should enable a relatively

The catcher's crouch

strong catcher to make an accurate throw to second base in order to throw out the runner.

On an attempted steal of third, of course, the catcher's feet spring up in the direction of third base in preparation for the throw.

A high foul pop-up, conversely, often provides the catcher with enough time to strip off the mask. In fact, you should train your catcher to always strip off the mask in the case of a foul ball or a wild pitch. It's difficult to search for the ball when wearing a mask because it severely limits the peripheral field of vision. The action should be fast, and it should coincide with the catcher springing from the crouch. Toss the mask in any direction away from the field—get it far out of the way and try to avoid it blocking the base paths or entering the field of play.

In addition to staying close to the plate, the catcher helps the pitcher by framing any pitch that may be near the boundaries of the strike zone. If it's a clear strike, and no base runner is advancing, the catcher should freeze his mitt for one or two seconds to allow

Catcher's free hand with runner on base

the umpire to make the correct call. If the pitch is closer to a ball, however, then the catcher needs to learn how to create the image of a strike for the umpire. In other words, he has to frame the pitch. On a pitch that's low, therefore, the catcher should snag the ball from the top and then angle his wrist up. On a high pitch, he catches it and then immediately lets his wrist drop into the strike zone. If it's inside on a right-handed batter, the catcher angles his glove with the open face toward the plate; on an outside pitch to a righty, he similarly angles the glove toward the plate but in a somewhat backhanded manner. After such catches, the catcher should slyly and subtly sneak the glove back into the strike zone before the umpire makes his call.

One of the most difficult plays for a catcher is when the pitch is in the dirt. Some catchers have remarkably fast hands, and these kids will tend to try to catch these balls on a hop. It's an impressive move when done well, but it's more effective to teach your catchers to instead drop to their knees to block such pitches so that the ball stays in front. A base runner in youth baseball will almost always

Catcher springs up

Catcher's move to throw out runner

take off if the pitch gets behind the catcher, and in most cases he'll be safe. But only the fastest and most daring runners will attempt to steal when the catcher manages to keep a wild throw in front of him and within his clear field of vision.

When blocking a pitch with base runners on, the catcher should place himself in the line of the throw, on his knees, and keep his body slightly hunched to cushion both the impact of the ball and the extent of the potential rebound. The glove should drop down low, and the throwing hand is best positioned near the glove. The catcher should then allow the ball to hit his body and not try to catch it (hard for a young, proud catcher to do). When executed well, the ball will drop somewhere in front of the catcher. He then springs up, recovers the ball, and either throws the runner out or threatens him back to his original base.

Another skill that's necessary to teach—because it's a play where the game is often on the line—is the preparation for a play at the plate. The catcher cannot block the plate without possession of the ball, but he can certainly do so if he has the ball or is about to receive

Catcher strips off mask

the throw. In such cases, the catcher, mask off, will be on one knee with the grounded knee and leg blocking the runner's access to the plate. Once the catcher has possession of the ball, of course, he has to protect it. There are different methods to do this, but one of the simplest approaches is to teach the catcher to hold the ball with his throwing hand inside of the glove, as the glove is tucked somewhat close to the chest. The tag can be applied to a sliding runner with both the throwing hand and the glove holding fast to the ball. In such cases, the catcher should always tag low (toward the legs) and never high. On the other hand, if the runner doesn't slide and instead barrels into the catcher, the catcher pulls the ball and glove close to his chest and more or less goes down with the impact while still holding the ball.

As your players age, it's a good idea for you to put only your toughest and smartest kids behind the plate!

Catcher blocks the plate and tags runner

9

DEFENSIVE STRATEGIES

If defense wins ballgames, nowhere is that more true than in youth baseball. In many cases, the team that makes the fewest errors is the team that ends up victorious. Maybe it's because hitting is relatively easier to teach than fielding. Or it may be that kids are more motivated to hit well than to field well. It could be a combination of both, plus the fact that a lot of coaches either tend to pick players in the draft that they know can hit or don't spend enough time on the more complex fielding and pitching fundamentals. In any event, there are a few basic defensive strategy tips that youth baseball coaches should always keep in mind.

First and foremost, teach your players, especially at the younger age levels, to get the sure out. If your players are young and still learning, have the fielders on the right side always throw to first to get the out even when there's a runner on second. Your shortstop and second baseman alone should work on getting a force at second, but for the most part you'll win ballgames at this younger level by having the kids make the easy play.

To some extent, this even holds true at the eleven- and twelve-year-old levels. If an easy out can be made, your infield should make it. However, if your infield, and especially your shortstop, is sharp, then get the lead runner, or even attempt a double play on a hard hit and well-fielded ground ball. You'll know as your players develop when they're capable of more sophisticated plays, and you should challenge them as soon as you think they're ready.

Second, drill your fielders with the idea that they can't throw the runner out if they haven't first cleanly fielded the hit ball. You see this type of error both from the kids throwing the ball and catching it. The throwers, who typically are about to field a grounder with runners on base, will start the process of throwing the ball before they really have possession of it in their gloves. They're anxious to make the play, and maybe they've watched Jose Reyes too much on TV. The play at the youth baseball level does not usually have to be "bang-bang." In practice, encourage your players to focus on catching the ball and then taking the time to throw it correctly. On the other end, the basemen charged with the job of catching the throw often unnecessarily miss a throw because, usually, they doggedly don't want to come off of the bag. Again, at practice, train your players to forget about the runner in this context and to remove their foot from the base if they have to make a play on an errant throw. This is an especially crucial skill for first basemen to master.

A large part of defensive strategy consists of where you position your fielders from batter to batter, depending on the game situation at hand. In general, youth baseball players, at least below the age of ten or eleven, tend to not pull the ball. For that reason, it's safe to have your shortstop positioned closer to second base and your second baseman closer than usual to first. With a runner on base, however, and the threat of a steal, both your shortstop and your second baseman need to be a lot closer to second base in order to take a throw from the catcher. With a runner only on first, your shortstop should take the throw at second, and your second baseman backs him up. That back-up, incidentally, should be at least ten feet behind the base. Also teach your center fielder to run in on a steal of second. If the ball gets away, and the center fielder is charging, there's a chance to throw that runner out at third or perhaps make him hesitant to run.

Your third baseman, depending on the age of your division and the level of play of the batter, is typically positioned somewhat off of the bag in the direction of the shortstop. However, if a pull hitter is up, then have that third baseman guard the line. It's advantageous also to teach your third basemen to guard the line in the younger divisions—eight or below. At that level, a sharply hit ball down the third base line is an instant double because left fielders aren't usually adept enough to run over in time and throw the ball back in. If a hit gets through the hole between the third baseman and the shortstop, however, it often will be limited to a single because the left fielder will be in a position to field it.

Also, always have your third baseman shy toward the bag with a runner on second who's threatening to steal. Obviously, the third baseman will take the throw on a steal from the catcher, but here he should be backed up by the shortstop (as long as there's no runner on first). In case the shortstop has to cover second when there's a steal of third, then the leftfielder should charge in to back up the play.

Double steals are more common in youth baseball than they are in the major leagues. On a double-steal, the second baseman ideally should cover second base, with backup from the center fielder; the third baseman covers third with backup from the shortstop. The reason you want to deploy the shortstop in this way, on this play, is because the catcher will try to get the lead runner. An overthrow at third has to be adequately backed up because an errant throw will result in a run scored.

Your outfielders become increasingly important as the kids you coach start to get older. At the younger levels, the outfielders tend to be your least capable players because your best fielders are normally deployed in the infield—where most of the action is. Your outfielders, however, certainly will have plays to make. There are usually four outfielders (a left fielder, a left center fielder, a right center fielder, and a right fielder) for divisions at age ten and below, and three outfielders for eleven- and twelve-year-olds. Besides learning how to catch fly balls, of course, your outfielders have particular skills to practice. Not the least of these includes hitting the cut-off man.

Just about every kid that plays the outfield understands the concept of hitting the cut-off man. However, when a ball is hit into the outfield they sometimes panic and forget what to do. Sometimes they even hand the ball over to the adjacent outfielder to decide what to do. Sometimes they fling it in the general direction of the infield but not close to any fielder. To keep things simple, train your left and right center fielder to throw the ball in to the second baseman. Your left and left center fielder should throw to the shortstop. If there's a runner on second, the left fielder should either know to throw it to the third baseman or be directed by the shortstop to do so. You need to practice hitting the cutoff man over and over during your practices. It's the only way your least-experienced players will come to do the right thing once that crucial moment arrives in a game.

As for the cutoff men themselves, you must train your shortstop and second baseman to go out onto the outfield grass to get the throw. Most younger outfielders won't throw as well as your infielders, so your infielders need to cut down the length of the outfield throw by creeping out onto the grass. At the older youth baseball ages, of course, this becomes less of a concern, but still that cut-off man should make it easier on the outfielders. Although the older kids will have stronger arms, they're also typically playing on deeper fields that require longer throws.

If your outfielders aren't good baseball players yet, it's a smart idea to place them a bit deeper in the outfield than you would position more capable players. If they're unlikely to catch a ball hit in the air to the outfield, then it's better if it lands in front of them, rather than behind them. Play them deep, and continue to teach them how to hit the cut-off man.

Another good technique for your outfielders to learn is to field ground balls to the outfield on one knee when no one is on base and no obvious play is to be made. Infielders never have to do this, because they're always backed up by the outfielders. But the outfielders are backed up by nothing but the outfield fence, so they have to be extra sure to make the stop.

On a play at the plate, the catcher decides whether the throw from the outfield should be cut off. He needs to be loud, and you need to train your catcher to be aggressively in charge. He's your captain on the field, and plays that involve him should defer to his command.

Young players also need to learn how to call for pop ups. At the younger ages, you may find that everyone in the infield calls for a ball hit in the air. You need to drill this a lot in practice—not only will proper execution prevent errors, but it will also prevent injuries. Basically, on a pop-up to the left side or middle of the field, the shortstop will call off both the second and third baseman if he thinks he can reach it. On a play to the right side, the second baseman calls off the first baseman. A pop-up to the mound, at least in youth baseball, is the pitcher's domain. And, again, any play that might involve the catcher is the catcher's decision over all.

The catcher also is the captain when it comes to fielding a bunt, because he's the only player who sees the entire field in front of him. Either he fields it, or he should decide which fielder does. If the first baseman takes the bunt, then the second baseman has to cover first. In the rare situations in youth baseball when you might expect a bunt, then the third baseman and first baseman generally should creep in toward the batter prior to the pitch.

A great defensive strategy to throw out a runner attempting to steal home also centers on the catcher. Here, with runners on first and third, the runner on first generally has an easy steal of second because catchers are hesitant to throw down since the runner on third will take off on the throw. Instead, on the catcher's sign to the shortstop, the catcher will throw to him, at the shortstop position, as the runner from first takes off. The key here is for the catcher to spring up and act like he's throwing to second base—this will cause the runner on third to take off for home. But instead of throwing it down to second, he surrenders that base and pegs the throw to the shortstop, who immediately returns the ball to the plate. If the catcher is in good position, and the throw back is accurate, that lead runner will almost always be thrown out at home. If coaches and catchers employ this strategy early in the game, opposing teams are far less likely to try to take second on a similar play later in the game.

There are also situations in youth baseball where both the infield and the outfield should play in. The classic situation concerning the infield, of course, would be late in a close game with a runner on third. In such a case, in anticipation of a play at the plate, the infield should step up onto the infield grass in order to quickly field a ground ball and throw it home. Moreover, with the game on the line in the bottom of the sixth inning, the outfield should play very shallow as well. If either a hit or a sacrifice fly is going to win the game, it makes sense to have the outfield play in close because almost no recreational youth baseball player is going to throw a runner out at the plate from deep in the outfield.

Some coaches at the older age levels like to play outfield defensive shifts on left-handed batters. In such scenarios, the center fielder moves over to left center, and the right fielder moves as far over as straightaway center field. The second baseman—the player now closest to covering right field—will play deep on the outfield grass. Unless you're very certain about the batter's propensity to pull, and to hit for power, such shifts are generally an example of over-coaching. Still, be aware that this sort of strategy is, under some circumstances, a relatively useful weapon in your defensive arsenal.

A final defensive strategy to practice is the rundown. The good news is that kids love to practice rundowns and will even spend extra time after practice, on their own, playing "running bases." So even though a rundown is a fairly complex play, youth baseball players in fact have a lot of practice executing it. The proper procedure involves four fielders, two at each base, to nail the runner.

If the rundown's between third and home, then the primary fielders are the third baseman and the catcher, backed up by the shortstop (at third) and pitcher (at home); if between second and third, the primary fielders are the shortstop and third baseman, backed up by the second baseman (at second) and the pitcher (at third); and, if between first and second, the primary fielders are the first baseman and the second baseman, backed up by the pitcher (at first) and the shortstop (at second). The essential drills are that both bases must be covered by someone at all times, and that the runner should always be chased back to the base he came from. Ideally, the ball should be thrown to the fielder covering that starting base when the runner retreats to about twenty feet from the base. At that point, the fielder who made the throw should circle out of the base path and rotate to back up the base he was charging toward. His backup fielder then advances and becomes the primary fielder in case the ball has to be returned. It's key to remind your players that the ball always must be thrown to the fielder at the base—and not to any fielder off the base or otherwise getting in the way. Accordingly, while one primary fielder is chasing the runner back, his counterpart must be waiting for the throw *at the base* and not somewhere down the line from it. When executed correctly, your four fielders continuously cycle in and out of the play, with the bases always being covered, until the runner is eventually either tagged out or safely reaches his original base on a fielding error.

The other main area of defense, of course, concerns your pitching. In youth baseball, however, there are limited pitching strategies you can employ short of having a pitcher who can throw strikes. For example, intentional walks are frowned upon and even prohibited in many leagues.

The most important strategy you can employ, however, pertains to how many successful pitchers you can develop. On a team of twelve players, it's not a stretch to try to develop as many as ten pitchers.

Some kids just won't want to pitch, and that's perfectly fine—there's no need to push them.

When your pitcher is struggling you sometimes just need to take a walk to the mound to encourage him. A lot of kids put too much pressure on themselves. Rather than shout at them or say something inane like, "throw some strikes," there are times when you just need to get them to relax. Sometimes just give them a piece of gum and ask them what they're planning to do over the summer—anything but the game. At the end of the little chat, slap them on the back and tell them you have full confidence in their ability to get the job done.

There are other times, especially in the heat of a playoff game or when your pitcher seems to be pitching scared, that you should be more direct. You can tell when a pitcher is aiming instead of just throwing—when you see that, you'll know that he's losing his confidence and his fight. At such times you have to go out there and remind him what he has inside. Remind him that you put him there because you believe in him. Remind him that he's your ace because he has the most guts on the team. Encourage him to dig down at those moments and find something he never thought he had. At such times, children want to be courageous, they want to be heroic—they will inevitably bear down and fight.

There are also times, of course, when you see a hitch in the pitcher's delivery, or a technical problem that can easily be fixed. Get out there then and tell your pitcher what to do—kick his leg higher, don't grip the ball so tightly, etc. The smallest adjustment sometimes puts a pitcher right back on track.

Then, of course, there are those times when all the wheels obviously are coming off. In those situations—both to keep your team in the game and to protect your pitcher's now-shaky confidence—you've got to take him off of the mound. This may or may not occur before your pitcher reaches your league's pitch count limit, but don't hesitate to pull him if he just doesn't have his stuff. You should have a game plan at least three or four pitchers deep with respect to who comes in next. Some players pitch more effectively as starters, and others as relievers—know who these kids are. Make sure, as well, that your backup pitchers know that they might get into that day's game in later innings so they can be emotionally prepared. Good pitching is a priceless premium in youth baseball. There are pitch counts to juggle, and there are pitchers that won't be available for certain games, so you need as much pitching as you can develop.

Luckily, a surprising majority of players, including those who barely throw well, can see themselves on the mound. Take all those kids, at whichever age level, and teach them how to pitch. Furthermore, put them all in a game at some point during the season. If you know some of these kids are unable to throw strikes, then give them two batters to prove you wrong. Again, one of the beauty's of youth baseball is the game's inherent ability to challenges its players. Don't hide away your least capable players. Put them in situations that appropriately challenge them without unduly sacrificing your team's chances to win. The worst that might happen is that you discover a player who has an ability, and a contribution to make, that neither he nor you ever knew he had.

10

NURTURING THE BOTTOM OF YOUR LINEUP

Unfortunately, the most radical concept in youth baseball today is the following: the bottom of your lineup is the most important part of your team.

The reason why this is true should be clear. Every recreational youth baseball coach has some good players, but every coach, virtually without exception, will have at least three kids who, at the start of the season, don't play especially well. The coach that over the course of ten to twelve games can get these players to hit and field reasonably well will succeed because (1) he will win more games, and (2) he will infuse his team with the joy that the least capable of players always generate when they, sometimes to their own surprise, succeed.

Many coaches, especially at the older age divisions, will ignore these players, feeling that they're either instant outs or need to be hidden away to do the least damage. But you've got only eighteen outs per game to burn in youth baseball, and you can't be content to easily sacrifice four to eight of them because it's not worth your time to properly teach a player how to hit.

A lot of children enjoy playing baseball because they know that they're good at it. That's fantastic—you want to choose these players first when you draft because you obviously need kids with ability. But think about the children who want to play even though it's obvious to them, as well as to others, that they're not so good. Why are they there? Why do these kids put themselves in a position where they might be embarrassed or even teased? Because they adore the game. They love to play baseball—don't you also want to have kids like this on your team?

The bottom of your order is generally comprised of the sorts of children who want to learn. They come to practice. They listen to what the coach has to say, and they very much appreciate the attention. They may be awkward at first, or for whatever reason slow to learn, but the smart and successful coach will appreciate them just as much as he does the best player on the team. And if the coach sets the tone with respect to how the least capable players are treated, then the rest of the team will follow. If the coach is pulling for the bottom of the lineup, then the players will as well. But if the coach obviously doesn't ever let these kids bat more than once in a game— ever—the players aren't likely to offer much support either.

Everyone can learn how to hit. You and your assistant coaches should make it a priority to teach these three or four kids how to do so. Have your assistant coaches work with them individually. Take them through the basics—some of these kids don't start to play organized baseball until they're ten or eleven, so of course they're behind the players who have been around since their T-ball days. So start at the beginning with them. Teach them the basics of hitting as if they're seven or eight years old. Train them how to run the bases. Start with the running game, as mentioned throughout this book, and then get them to start hitting the ball. You'll typically have to correct their footwork in the batter's box; get them not to turn their heads when they swing; and prevent them from lunging at pitches, but they will eventually get it. They likely won't ever be as good as the best players on your team, but if they can make contact when they bat then the bottom of your lineup will be far ahead of the opposing teams in your division.

These players, of course, will spend the bulk of their fielding time in the outfield, but don't restrict them to right field. Introduce them to infield play by occasionally putting them at second base, or, if they have decent arms, at third. Second base is a great position to introduce your least experienced players to infield play because the throws from second to first are short, and also because your pitcher—typically one of the better players on your team—will handle some of the plays to the right side of the field and thus not totally expose that part of your defense. Train your least capable players to catch both grounders and fly balls. Teach them how to not be afraid of the ball, if that's a problem too. Everyone has to play at least a few innings in the field, at any level, so the coach that can coax something out of the bottom of his lineup has an enormous advantage over the other teams.

At the older levels of youth baseball, around eleven or twelve years old, coaches will be faced with the extra challenge of having as many as twelve or thirteen players under rules that allow only ten to bat in order. In other words, depending on your league's rules, a coach generally will be required to substitute in his least capable players for two or three innings in the field and at least one at-bat. This isn't easy to do, particularly in a playoff game, and especially where your least capable two or three players are demonstrably not as good as the rest of the team. Still, they have to play. More to the point, they are vitally important to your team, and the contributions they make in the playoffs, when it matters, will be a direct result of the abilities they developed and the confidence you nurtured within them earlier in the season. If you've buried a kid on the bench all season don't expect him to play second base well with the game on the line.

Take the worst players on your team and give them an identity. Make them your "Bulldogs," or your "Desperadoes"—whatever moniker best fits their particular personalities. As suggested earlier, have them lead the running drills, at least. Let them bat first during batting practice. Occasionally, give them a chance to pitch in a game, if they want to, or a time to bat first in the order. Especially at the older age levels, where players have to be substituted in and the bench typically has to play one or two innings in the field, have these players start a game once in awhile and give them their at-bats within the first two innings. From a strictly strategic perspective, you've gotten them in early and saved your best players for the late innings. But from a childhood development point of view, you've given your least confident players the chance to brag that they started and led off the game. This sort of encouragement, every once in a while, keeps not only these players but the parents of these players engaged and happy.

And these parents are crucial to you. They may be skeptical at first about how you intend to coach their kids. They will certainly be worried that their child won't play enough, won't have a good time and may be ostracized by the better players on the team. Further-more, for the most part, they won't be shy about letting you know that their kid deserves more playing time and attention.

Playing time, however, shouldn't be the issue, because the least capable players simply will get the least amount of playing time. Instead, the question is about consideration. Are you giving at least the same amount of attention to the kids at the bottom of your lineup that you give to your star player? A parent will know whether or not you are. And if you are, if you're working with his or her kid at practices to help him to improve, a parent will see that and generally not complain about playing time. But if you're ignoring the kid and wishing he were never on your team, a parent will see that too.

Every parent should understand that the better players will get the most playing time. That means that the coach should engage the parent of a player who may not yet be as good to help that player to become better. Practice time and field space, especially in urban areas, are at a premium. If a coach is lucky, in most cases, he'll find the time and space for two practices a week in addition to the one or two games per week on the schedule. If a child is to improve as a baseball player, however, what's needed is repetitive, daily practice. It's great for a coach to work with and give instructions to a less capable player; it's even better for that kid to play catch with a parent on the other days when the team isn't either practicing or playing. Engage your parents to do this, if possible.

Give the players at the bottom of your order appropriate expectations. They don't need to become ace pitchers or regular first basemen by the end of the season. Rather, encourage them to make contact when they bat, throw the ball effectively, and learn how to catch the ball with few errors. Any of your lowest draft choices that can do this are huge advantages for your team.

Also keenly observe their strengths and weaknesses. If a player hits reasonably well but his fielding still needs work, then put him at designated hitter if your league allows that. If a player fields ground balls fairly well but has a weak arm, then try him at second base instead of the outfield. Be flexible. And, most importantly, listen to that player when he has any question or concern.

There are huge payoffs to engaging the bottom of your order. The joy that these kids have when they get a hit or catch a ball is, without exception, infectious. Their successes rouse the team and lift everyone's spirits. If the bottom of your order hits, then the top of your order gets more at bats. If the bottom of your order hits, the top of your order will drive them in.

More importantly, you, as a coach, are in a unique position to contribute to a child's emotional development. A lot of coaches think that their mission is to win the championship. Still others have the notion that they're there to prepare only the very best players to go on to play high school ball—in other words, in essence, the rest of the team really doesn't matter. Others, although they won't admit it, coach just so their own kids are provided the opportunities to play the choicest positions and be selected for the all-star and regional tournaments. This sort of coach, regrettably, might be the worst of all.

Youth baseball, in so many ways, is an emotional battlefield for children. It serves a modern-day role similar to what you might imagine early hunting expeditions did for young boys in native cultures. It's the relatively safe training ground for children to test their early mettle. It's a place for them to learn how to respond under pressure, to discover how to deal with defeat, and to experience what sort of courage they're capable of summoning up when the crucial moment comes and everyone that they care about is watching. A coach that coddles his own son deprives him of all that. If you indulge your child on the baseball field, no matter how good he may be, you will end up with a spoiled brat.

Time and again this happens, however. And while that kid is proud of his accomplishments at the ages of eight, nine or ten, he starts to observe by the time that he's eleven or twelve that it's actually been his father that has constantly had his back. Deep inside, that child knows this, and his confidence is lacking. You can tell who this kid is because he's the one who cries when he strikes out. He's the one who needs his father, the coach, to bail him out after being ejected from a game for poor sportsmanship.

At the other extreme, and something perhaps even more coaches need to guard against, is the tendency to treat your own son more harshly than your other players. Sometimes coaches ride their sons so hard and humiliate them in the middle of the game, in front of their peers. These at-times blistering denunciations are hard not only for the other children, but even for the surrounding adults, to hear. The child, often taking the abuse while standing at his position in the field, tries to shut it out and pretends to ignore his father/coach, which only makes the father/coach more irate. This abuse, often precipitated by something as excusable as missing a hard-hit ball, doesn't make your son tougher, and it certainly won't make him play better. He already feels bad, and having his father chastise him in front of his friends is a nightmare. If anything, it will make him walk away from the game—and possibly from you, as well—as he gets older. Coaches need to keep this anger, at least publicly, very much in check.

So in contrast to the coach's children, sometimes, the kids at the bottom of the lineup tend to be more emotionally sound. They're used to failure, and they know how to deal with it. And when they win, when things occasionally go their way—as they will, their joy is boundless.

As a coach and, moreover, as a parent, who would you rather help to nurture at the end of the day? A decent high school baseball player who's fundamentally weak inside, or a kid who does his best and, as a result of challenging himself, is also emotionally strong? It's an important question to ask, because there's so much more at stake when coaching youth baseball than simply learning how to hit a ball with a bat.

11

HOW TO COMMUNICATE WITH BAD UMPIRES AND ZEALOUS PARENTS

Everyone has always hated the ump. As far back as the 1880s, when umpires were first paid to call professional baseball games, their lives were at stake. At Opening Day at New York's Polo Grounds in 1884, where the forerunners of the San Francisco Giants squared off at home against the ancestors of the Chicago Cubs, a crowd of 10,000 fans, disappointed with the quality of the game-calling, broke through a grandstand enclosure in the late innings and rioted on the field. According to the next day's news reports, someone threw a seat cushion in the air and soon thousands of cushions followed. After the "air was filled with the missiles for many minutes," and an umpire "was hissed, and threats were made of doing him bodily harm," order was eventually restored and the game continued.

Twenty-first century youth baseball games can be somewhat similar affairs. Depending on how close the crowd is to the action, bad umpires—often volunteer parents—can easily lose control of a game. Of course these umpires, whether paid by the league or volunteers, don't set out to be bad. Rather, they may be inexperienced or just subject to the same human error that we're all affected by. The problem is that they're expected to be perfect. A more difficult challenge is that the bad calls often are exacerbated by poor reactions from coaches and their players.

How a coach and his players deal with a bad call can affect not only the rest of the game but also a season. You've got to be diplomatic and, under all circumstances, maintain self-control. Essentially, don't act like the stereotypical Billy Martin. Don't get in an umpire's face, don't kick dirt, don't embarrass and humiliate him, and don't argue balls and strikes from the dugout or base coach box. Don't continue to argue the call after play has resumed. And maybe this should be obvious, but never curse at the umpire—or curse at all, for that matter—in front of your players.

Remember that almost all umpires love the game too, and they are doing their best. Most of the bad calls, of course, are matters of interpretation—balls and strikes near the corners, the so-called tie-goes-to-the-runner rule, close plays at home or third base. And many youth baseball games have only one umpire, or at most two. It's extremely difficult to call a close tag at second base when you're standing behind the catcher with a mask on. Calls at third, including missed tags, are also very hard to see unless you're positioned directly behind the bag. Mistakes will be made even by the most experienced and conscientious umps.

The key for coaches and players—and really the only control you have over bad umpiring—is how you relate and react to the umpire and his calls. You have to be civil. If nothing else, your lack of civility will result in more calls going against you throughout the game.

For one thing, you should coach your players about how to react to calls they disagree with. A lot of kids upon being called out on strikes stand in shock at the plate and motion to you, in the dugout, to somehow do something about the travesty that just befell them. Ignore this, of course, and get that player back in the dugout once the at-bat is over. Generally, just don't argue balls and strikes. You won't win, you're not behind the plate and can't really be sure that the call was bad, and you'll only waste your good will with the umpire when you might need it on a more crucial play. If you feel the need to discuss a call with an umpire, make it a quiet conversation and never show him up in front of his umpiring peers.

Respect the umpires. Greet them before the game, engage them in small talk and find out what sort of a strike zone they plan to call. If it's a tight one, then let your pitchers and all your hitters know it. As long as the umpire's calls are consistent, there's really nothing to argue about. If your pitcher feels the need to complain about it, he really just has to throw better strikes. The other team, presumably, is dealing with the same strike zone too.

Your best ambassador to the home plate ump is your catcher. Among the many important duties the catcher has is to establish very good relations with the umpire. And among all your hitters, he especially should never argue balls and strikes when he's batting. If the pitcher seems frustrated by the umpire's strike zone, your catcher should ask about it and then go discuss the matter with your pitcher. This creates the appearance for the umpire that your battery is working to throw the strikes where he, the umpire, prefers to see them. A good relationship between your catcher and the umpire will definitely result in at least some close calls going your way. If the umpire is fond of your catcher, he'll call strikes on the near misses that your catcher manages to frame well.

Your players, of course, are children, but they should nevertheless be coached to not engage in disruptive or unsportsmanlike conduct toward the umpire. This means that they shouldn't throw helmets, flip a bat or give cold stares to the ump after a call. And if your player is ejected as a result of such disproportionately bad behavior, you, as a coach, ought to support that call. Help that kid to pack his stuff and send him home.

At the same time, you have to gauge your players' emotions to see how they deal with bad calls, or generally how they deal with things not going their way. Do they pout? Do they kick equipment in the dugout? If so, then you need to discipline them in a way that you, as coach, know is best for that particular player. If they refrain from such poor behaviors, and instead forget about the call and get back to work, then you've got the makings of a well-controlled, contributive ballplayer.

If you lose your cool as a coach—and it does happen on some especially egregious calls—be sure to apologize to the umpire after the game and, if necessary, apologize to your team as well. They'll appreciate that you made a mistake and owned up to it. What constitutes an egregious call? Taking away a home run from a young player who had never hit one seems to qualify, when the hit is discounted as a result of a failure to touch a base during his circuit. It's technically the right call, of course, but it's bad form for an opposing coach to challenge it, and it is a pretty rough message for an eight-year-old to take—especially when there's some dispute about whether or not it actually happened. But, again, close plays and balls and strikes generally have to be left alone.

When a game is called well, the umpires fade into the background. Congratulate and thank them after they call such a game—it's always to the benefit of the kids when everyone works together on their behalf. And once you've mastered the art of dealing with umpires, you're ready for the ultimate test: overzealous parents.

Of course most of the parents of your players will be terrific people. If they see that you care about the team, and particularly about their kids, then you'll have no problems. Other sorts of parents are not as helpful: the ones that come onto the field during the game to give unsolicited advice; the ones who position themselves more as agents than parents to their children; the ones who can't manage to get their kids to practice on time; the ones that complain loudly about all the other players apart from their own kid; and the ones who nag you because they think their child should be batting higher in the order and playing in more key positions.

You have to try to always keep it light with these parents. Stay casual with them and use humor to your best advantage, even if they're driving you crazy inside. Draw the line, though, when they start to encroach your responsibilities on the field. In fact, make it clear, in a nice way, that they're not welcome on the field.

It's important, of course, to have an assistant coach keep a detailed scorecard during your games and also compile all the stats for the players throughout the season. For pitchers, you should at least keep track of innings pitched, hits allowed, walks, strikeouts and WHIP (walks plus hits per innings pitched). For your hitters, compile at-bats, hits, strikeouts, runs scored, walks, doubles, triples, home runs, RBIs, stolen bases, reached on error, batting average and on-base percentage. Not only are these numbers vital to understanding your players' performances, and to adjust your batting orders accordingly, but they also come in very handy when a parent complains that their son or daughter shouldn't be batting ninth or tenth. You can back up your decisions by showing the parent their kids' numbers. Moreover, why not invite that parent to keep score during the games? Most coaches could always use more assistant coaching help, and by recording the performances of all the players, the parent will get a realistic view of how all the children are performing and how you are functioning as coach.

There's not much you can, or should, do about parents who sit in the bleachers and grumble about you or the performance of the players other than their own kid. People will tell you about these comments but just shrug them off. Whatever you're hearing is hearsay, and you'll only create more problems by confronting the alleged complainers. If it bothers the people on the bleachers, let the people on the bleachers take care of it.

The parents of the prima donna players are in a class of their own. A lot of times dealing with these parents is more like talking to a player's agent. They may tell you that their kid might not be available for the game unless he's scheduled to start. They may not return phone calls or emails. It's hard to make a game plan, of course, if you never know if your best player is going to show up. These parents, and there are surprisingly many of them, don't look at youth baseball as an opportunity for their kids to have fun and maybe an ice cream cone after the game. Instead, they intend for you to help put Junior on the path to becoming one of the roughly 800 major league baseball players in the world. Patience and flattery works best in these cases. If you have to, be strict with that player on the field, but try to be gentle and feed the ego of the parent who you need to get that player to the game.

As for the parents who either don't bring their children to practice or can't seem to get them there on time: cajole them, beg them if you have to, but try to make them understand why the practices are so important. But whatever you do, never punish their player for being late—he or she wants to be there, and there is no point in reprimanding them. And when such parents don't bother to even stay to watch their own kids play—well, that's just very sad indeed.

Hopefully you'll never have to deal with parents like these. Instead, the vast majority of men and women come back to coach year after year because, in part, they've made so many friends with parents of their players. The great relationships you have the opportunity to establish through youth baseball far outweigh having to deal with an annoying parent or two. You're the Pied Piper to a gang of kids, and really just about all of these parents are rooting you on. It's amazing to see everyone get on board as the spirit of your team is forged and the kids start their run toward the playoffs. The end of the season can be almost overwhelming: the genuine thanks that many parents express to the coach are sometimes even embarrassing.

It may be that a team finally comes together when all the parents involved really start pulling in the same direction for the kids. Maybe it starts when the practices and games are understood by everyone as building blocks toward the shared goal of victory, instead of just more activities to deal with on someone's busy schedule. Or it may be when not only the players but the parents, too, share the burdens of team interdependence. Or when the commitment of the son or daughter inspires equal devotion from mom and dad. Or it could be when everyone involved in supporting the team honestly shares the burdens of accountability—win or lose.

It's never clear from year to year what causes the spark that lights up a successful team, but you'll feel it when it happens. It all comes down to how far you've pulled back that arrow in the bow before letting it fly: your consideration of each and every last player, your efforts to practice and to teach throughout the season. It may come late, or it may not even occur until you're deep in the playoffs, but there's a very palpable change when your team goes from a disparate group of kids who may or may not be familiar with each other to one with a collective identity and spirit. That's when the games become not only fun but truly memorable. At the end of the day, no one will recall specific scores. But they'll remember that a certain season was epic. And the kids you do reach, without any regard to their baseball abilities, will at least vaguely recall what kind of man or woman you were.

TWELVE-PLUS WAYS TO HAVE FUN ON A BASEBALL FIELD

Along with the various drills already described, the following twelve (plus one) drills are effective and fun ways to both teach your players essential baseball skills and keep them fully engaged during practices. There's no way to employ all of these drills at every practice, but you should regularly cycle through them—and others that you or fellow coaches may have developed—to keep your team sharp and skilled.

1. The Around-the-Horn Drill

This is an infield drill. Position a player at each infield position, including catcher, but not at pitcher. Any extra players should line up behind the shortstop. The coach hits a ground ball to the shortstop, who throws to first. The first baseman then rifles the ball across the diamond to the third baseman. The third baseman gets it, and then throws it in to the catcher, who hands the ball back to the coach. At the end of this circuit, all the players rotate around the horn:

the first baseman covers second, the second baseman goes to third, the third baseman covers catcher, the shortstop takes first base, and the catcher goes to the end of the shortstop line. The next shortstop then steps forward to take the grounder. As your players improve, the drill should be conducted at an increasing speed, with the fielders rotating their positions as soon as their plays are completed. If you have fewer players, such as five, the drill can be made more interesting by keeping the individual scores of errors or dropped plays.

2. The Lacrosse Stick Drill

A lacrosse stick, for some reason, comes as close to mimicking the feel off the bat of a deep fly ball as anything else. And unless you or your assistant coaches can hit deep fly ball fungoes with any accurate regularity, this is a great tool for outfield practices. Line up your outfielders two or three deep in right, center and left. Have an additional player positioned at second, and also one at shortstop. Standing at the plate (or on the mound if you need to move up), fling the baseball in the lacrosse stick in the general direction of your outfielders. Have them practice both coming in and going back on the ball. In all cases, they should return the ball to the appropriate cutoff man at either second or short. Alternatively, place two buckets in the positions where the cutoff men would be and direct the outfielders to try to return the caught balls to the buckets. You can assign them descending points based on whether they land it in the bucket on a fly; whether they hit it on a fly; or whether they strike it on a bounce. The lacrosse stick will enable you to fire the balls at will, so the drill should be rapid and move from right to center to left very quickly. Everyone needs to be on their toes (literally and figuratively), and the infielders roll the balls back to you after they've been retrieved.

3. The Don't Make Me Move Drill

This is a fun outfield drill for younger players. Array your squad (or half of your squad) in the outfield, with their gloves on, and take a position in front of them at a distance where all should be able to reasonably reach you on a fly. Call a player's name and throw him a ball either on the ground or in the air. The player then has to field it cleanly and throw it back to you on either a fly or on one bounce, and accurate enough so that you don't have to move your feet to field it. If the ball either reaches you on more than one bounce, or if you're compelled to move both of your feet to your right or left to field it, then that player is out. Continue the game until there's only one player standing.

4. The Bottle-Cap Drill

This drill provides your players with a surprisingly satisfying sense of accomplishment, even though they end up hitting little plastic targets no more than a few feet. You can run this drill by splitting the squad into pitchers and hitters, and you can do this anywhere on the field. All you need to be prepared is a few dozen plastic bottle caps. Pair off your pitchers and hitters, and be sure to position your hitters, with their bats, a safe distance away from each other. Distribute your caps among the pitchers, and have them stand no more than a few feet away from the hitters. They should then toss the caps one by one to the hitters. Hitting a bottle cap isn't especially easy at first, but the batters will adjust, and soon they'll be swinging hard in an attempt to get it back to the pitcher or possibly to crack the darn thing. After about twenty swings, the pitchers and hitters switch. Obviously, this drill focuses the hitter's attention on a very small target. When they next see live pitching, the baseball will comparably look like a beach ball to the batter.

5. Base Running Relays

This drill reinforces proper base running, but it puts it in a competitive context that keeps your players motivated. Split your squad into two groups. Put one group in a line behind second base, and the other in a line at home. Give each team one baseball. At the sound of a whistle, the lead runners in each group take off—the runner on second toward third, around home, and then past first back to second; the runner at home toward first, second, third and then home. When the respective runners reach their destinations (second or home), the next runner takes the relay baseball and takes off. The coaches need to watch to make sure the runners are hitting each base and that the opposing team doesn't touch or interfere with the runners. Whichever team finishes first wins. If any runner missed a base, however, then his or her team is disqualified. You can mix up the drill and continue to play it by switching around a couple of players on each team after every relay.

6. The Five-on-Five

Split the squad into five players each and play a three-inning scrimmage, with two outs per half-inning instead of three. A coach will serve as the designated pitcher, and any additional coaches or parents can man the outfield positions. There is no catcher position, and no stealing is allowed. The five-on-five is essentially an abbreviated game that's useful, especially if you're pressed for time, because each player will likely end up with a few at-bats and everyone also will get chances in the infield. But beware: you'll be amazed at how competitive kids on the same baseball team will become when they're suddenly facing off against a half-squad of their very own team.

7. Situational Running/Fielding Drills

It's very important to train both your infielders and your base runners to think instinctively in the heat of a game. The only way to do this, of course, is to drill it into them at practice. Situational base running drills are extremely important. For this particular drill, you'll need each of your infielders, plus a pitcher on the mound, and two base runners. Establish for them the scenario—usually a no-out or one-out situation—and vary the runners on base. For example: move from a man on second, to first and second on the next play; mix in a runner on second with two outs; go back to first and second and hit a grounder to first; create a play where the pitcher should cover first. Also useful is the practice of fielding double plays without mitts. Softly toss a grounder to your short-stop, who should recover it with both hands and then throw to the second baseman, who likewise should catch it with both hands and fire it on to first. The purpose of this particular drill is to teach your infielders to use both hands—especially whichever fielder takes the throw at second—because those double-play partners need to establish very quick releases to get the runner at first. Rather than transferring the ball from glove to hand, the second baseman who trains himself to catch it with both hands has saved himself precious time during a game.

8. The Rundown

Although kids love to play running bases on their own, you still need to drill them on correct execution because mistakes will be made under real-game pressure. Again, split the squad into two groups. Have one coach take five players—four fielders and a runner between first and second, and a second coach can work between third and home. Without placing too much focus on exactly which position player should be covering where, randomly place two players at each base, and have your runner take a long lead at either first or third. The primary first baseman and third baseman should each have a ball. When the coach blows a whistle, the runner starts to run toward the next base. The fielder with the ball will give chase, with the ball held high above his head with his throwing hand. By the time the runner is at full speed toward the next base, the fielder—let's say the first baseman—should throw to the other primary fielder and then circle to the line behind second base. That second baseman either tags or chases the runner back, as the next first baseman steps up. The players continue to cycle until either the runner is out or safe. At all times, whether in a game or at practice, make sure your fielders don't pump their arms to fake a throw. This can distract your other fielder and prevent him from anticipating when the real throw actually will be released.

9. The Tomahawk and Power-hand Drills

Coaches can perform these two drills fairly quickly with individual players. For the top-hand, or tomahawk drill, have your player hold the bat in a position to swing with only his top hand (e.g., the right hand for right-handed hitters). The coach soft tosses the ball from a close distance, and the player should try to tomahawk, or come down over the top of the ball so as to hit it into the dirt. After about twenty swings, the batter should switch to the bottom or power hand. Here, the batter will need to choke up on the bat, and he can either hit off of a tee or a soft toss. The batter should also stride and swing away at each toss as he would in a normal at bat. The batter, for balance, may have to place his free hand under the armpit of the swinging arm. An important coaching tip here is to observe whether the batter is lunging. If so, encourage him to stay back. The point of both drills is to isolate and develop proper technique and strength within each arm. Players also enjoy the challenge of trying to make contact with one arm.

10. Under the Bridge Tag

This is a game designed for younger players, but it begins to prepare them for a fundamental skill that will become important as they get older. Have all the players take a position anywhere in the infield, with their gloves. Ask them some sort of kid-appropriate trivia question (e.g., what is SpongeBob's job?) and shout it out. The kid who answers first is "it." That player then is given the ball and told to hold it in his glove. He then chases the others around the infield—no one can run past the baselines—and tags them out, but only if he or she uses the glove with the ball inside of it. The out player has to freeze on hands and feet until another player crawls under the "bridge" to free them. After a few minutes, or when the "it" player loses the ball from his glove, then another "it" is chosen and the play starts again.

Through this game, the players learn both how to tag and how to avoid being tagged.

11. The Fakeout

Also a drill for younger players, this game promotes quick reactions and good hands on grounders. Have your players surround you in a relatively tight circle with their gloves on. You should have a bucket of balls at your feet. Spontaneously toss grounders to any player, making them field at different glove positions and faking them out by not necessarily looking where you plan to throw. If the ball gets behind them, then that player's out, and the circle tightens. You can gradually make the drill more challenging by starting to toss out two or even three grounders at a time.

12. The Big Fat Ball Drill

This is a drill designed for younger players, but it can be useful for older players as well. Start by placing a soccer or volleyball on top of a batting tee (you may need to devise a ball holder or slip something like a plunger through the top of the tee to keep the ball balanced). Have the player hit the ball hard. They, of course, better not miss the ball, but what you're looking to see is whether they follow through with their swing. If that big fat ball doesn't explode off of the tee, then your player isn't driving through a baseball either. Since kids will be confident to swing at such a large target, the exercise offers you an easy look into their mechanics and will allow you to observe where adjustments might be needed.

BONUS: The Gatorade Bath

Prepare a large container of a pre-mixed sports drink on a very hot day, and keep it on the bench for your players to stay hydrated during the game. Win the championship. Make sure to act surprised when your son or daughter leads the charge and dumps the container on your head after the game. Reflect on how fun and rewarding it's been to coach youth baseball.

ACKNOWLEDGMENTS »

I wish to thank each one of the terrific kids I've had the pleasure to coach, because, among other things, they taught me more than I taught them. I also thank all of their parents, and the following individuals who generously helped me to complete this book: my editor Mark Weinstein, baseball coach extraordinaire Greg Polius, Wes and Isabella Padasak, Darrell and Zuri Watson, Manual Elias, Larry Florin, Elissa Jiji, Brian Krogman, Jennifer Lyons, Tom Walsh, Randy Wood, and Daisaku Ikeda. Finally, thank you to my wife, Jessica, who never complains that our home is stuffed with bats, balls and bases, or that our sons have turned the living room into their personal baseball diamond—and our own little field of dreams.

ABOUT THE AUTHOR »

Jeff Ourvan is an attorney, literary agent, and writer living in New York City. He has three sons and has coached their winning youth baseball teams as part of several New York-area leagues. For more "every kid wins" coaching tips, to contact Jeff, or to post your own youth coaching advice and experiences, visit http://www.everykidwins.com.

© David Bartolomi

INDEX »